KU-776-003

BEST OF

Madrid

Sally O'Brien

Best of Madrid
2nd edition – September 2005
First published – March 2003

Published by Lonely Planet Publications Pty Ltd
ABN 36 005 607 983

Australia	Head Office, Locked Bag 1, Footscray, Vic 3011
	☎ 03 8379 8000 fax 03 8379 8111
	🖳 talk2us@lonelyplanet.com.au
USA	150 Linden St, Oakland, CA 94607
	☎ 510 893 8555 toll free 800 275 8555
	fax 510 893 8572
	🖳 info@lonelyplanet.com
UK	72–82 Rosebery Avenue, London EC1R 4RW
	☎ 020 7841 9000 fax 020 7841 9001
	🖳 go@lonelyplanet.co.uk

This title was commissioned in Lonely Planet's London
office and produced by: **Commissioning Editor** Heather
Dickson, Stefanie Di Trocchio **Coordinating Editor** Imogen
Bannister **Coordinating Cartographer** Natasha Velleley
Layout Designer Sally Darmody **Editor** Kate Evans
Managing Cartographer Mark Griffiths **Cover Designer**
Sonya Brooke **Project Manager** Eoin Dunlevy **Mapping
Development** Paul Piaia **Thanks to** Kaitlin Beckett, Jovan
Djukanovic, Bruce Evans, Jacqui Saunders, John Shippick,
Glenn Cosby , Wayne Murphy

© Lonely Planet Publications Pty Ltd 2005.

Photographs by Lonely Planet Images and Richard
Nebeský except for the following: p7, p10, p11, p18, p20,
p22, p25, p27, p28, p33, p34, p40, p41, p43, p44, p45,
p48, p49, p51, p53, p56, p61, p66, p69, p73, p77, p78,
p79, p80 Guy Moberly, p35 Damien Simonis, p36 Jonathan
Chester, p37 Donald C & Priscilla Alexander Eastman.
Cover photograph Festival of San Isidro, Madrid, Aguililla
& Marin/Photolibrary. All images are copyright of the
photographers unless otherwise indicated. Many of the
images in this guide are available for licensing from
Lonely Planet Images: 🖳 www.lonelyplanetimages.com.

ISBN 1 74059 698 6

Printed by Markono Print Media Pte Ltd, Singapore

Acknowledgements © Madrid Metro Map © 2004 Metro
de Madrid SA

HOW TO USE THIS BOOK

Colour-Coding & Maps

Each chapter has a colour code along the
banner at the top of the page which is also
used for text and symbols on maps (eg all
venues reviewed in the Highlights chapter
are orange on the maps). The fold-out
maps inside the front and back covers are
numbered from 1 to 4. All sights and venues
in the text have map references; eg, (3, J5)
means Map 3, grid reference J5. See p96 for
map symbols.

Prices

Multiple prices listed with reviews (eg €10/5)
usually indicate adult/concession admission to
a venue. Concession prices can include senior,
student, member or coupon discounts. Meal
cost and room rate categories are listed at
the start of the Eating and Sleeping chapters,
respectively.

Text Symbols

☎	telephone
✉	address
🖳	email/website address
€	admission
☺	opening hours
ⓘ	information
Ⓜ	metro
🚆	cercanías
🚌	bus
♿	wheelchair access
✕	nonsmoking
✗	on-site/nearby eatery
♣	child-friendly venue
Ⓥ	good vegetarian selection

Contents

From the Publisher

AUTHOR

Sally O'Brien

Sally first visited Madrid as a teenager in the 1980s during the heady days of *la movida,* and fell in love with the art galleries, crazy little bars, streets seemingly paved with tapas and the city's extraordinary inhabitants. She's been back many times since, authoring the first and second editions of this title for Lonely Planet, and making plans to spend more time in the city she considers the best in the world.

Sally says *muchas gracias* to Heather Dickson for the work, Imogen Bannister for editing and Natasha Velleley for mapping this guide, Damien Simonis and Sarah Andrews for a brilliant city guide, Charo for the La Latina digs, Zoe for long semiliterary lunches, plus Jaime, Will, James, Matias, Amaia, and last but not least, my good friend and colleague Anthony Ham for the warm welcome, and his delightful wife Marina for charming company and a great translation service – you guys are the milk.

PHOTOGRAPHER

Richard Nebeský

Richard was born one snowy night in the grungy Prague suburb of Zizkov, but surprisingly he didn't have a camera in his hand. It was, however, not long after he got out of his cot that his father, an avid photo enthusiast, gave him his first point and shoot unit. Ever since, the camera has been by his side on wander treks, ski adventures, cycling trips and while researching Lonely Planet books around the globe. Richard has also worked for various magazines, travel publishers and many social photography projects. The magic of Madrid's architecture and the uniqueness of art works by Dalí and Picasso always draw him back. This time Richard's stay had a wonderful twist to it – the royal wedding.

SEND US YOUR FEEDBACK

We love to hear from travellers – your comments keep us on our toes and help make our books better. Our well-travelled team reads every word on what you loved or loathed about this book. Although we cannot reply individually to postal submissions, we always guarantee that your feedback goes straight to the appropriate authors, in time for the next edition – and the most useful submissions are rewarded with a free book. To send us your updates – and find out about Lonely Planet events, newsletters and travel news – visit our award-winning website: 🖳 **www.lonelyplanet.com/feedback.**

Note: We may edit, reproduce and incorporate your comments in Lonely Planet products such as guide-books, websites and digital products, so let us know if you don't want your comments reproduced or your name acknowledged. For a copy of our privacy policy visit 🖳 www.lonelyplanet.com/privacy.

Introducing Madrid

Madrid is a stamina-testing feast – it starts with a heady, frothy beer slammed down in front of you, is accompanied by a plate of tempting tit-bits pushed towards you, and then followed by numerous delicious courses that could be either traditional or inventive, before you find yourself dunking *churros* (doughnuts) into a perfect hot chocolate with a crowd of Madrileños at 6am.

And speaking of the locals, Madrid is full to bursting with people who pride themselves on an 'anything goes' attitude to other peoples' lives. The harsh repression of the Franco years saw an explosion of extroverted creativity and festivity upon his demise in 1975, and Madrileños aren't about to look back. Don't be surprised by animated conversations between strangers being struck up around you – join in. Self-consciousness and 'knowing one's place' are not the norm here – enjoying life is, whether it be at a sun-drenched *terraza* (terrace), a spine-tingling flamenco performance, a bloody bullfight, a star-studded soccer match, a long lunch, a quick tapas stop, a soul-stirring day in an art museum, early morning dancing in a nightclub or a colourful local fiesta.

Madrid is a city that propels itself ever-forward, but values its most civilised and passionately held traditions, such as the siesta and the local fiesta. She may be a European capital par excellence, but she's not about to lose her local flavour to the Eurocrats. Madrid is sweet, she's savoury and she's sometimes salty – but she's never bland. Make room for the best banquet in the world!

Feast your eyes upon the Palacio Real (p15), one small portion of the banquet that is Madrid

Neighbourhoods

Madrid is divided up into *distritos* (districts) and these are subdivided into barrios (neighbourhoods), the official names of which are largely ignored by locals. East of the Palacio Real lies the **Los Austrias** barrio, sometimes called the *morería,* or Moorish quarter, with charming narrow streets, traditional restaurants and Plaza Mayor.

A little southeast of this are the **La Latina** and **Lavapiés** barrios, which are rich examples of *castizo* (distinctly Madrid) life mixed with new waves of immigration.

Sol, **Huertas** and **Santa Ana** (to the east of Los Austrias) are *the* eating and drinking zones, with thousands of bars and big crowds at night. They were also the scene of the literary golden age in the 17th century.

North of Gran Vía lies the pink

Off the Beaten Track

The areas that feel most touristy in Madrid tend to surround Plaza de la Puerta del Sol and Plaza Mayor, or the 'big three' art museums. For the most part, La Latina, Lavapiés, Chueca and Malasaña remain faithfully local haunts, except at night, when Madrid becomes a mobile party town. The city's parks are also good places to escape to during the week.

barrio of **Chueca**, a respectable 19th-century area that fell on hard times and has been rejuvenated by the gay community. West of this is **Malasaña**, once a working-class district and now popular for nightlife, with a bohemian feel. Further west, you'll find middle class **Argüelles**, with pleasant *terrazas* (terraces) and a distinctly untouristed feel. North of Malasaña is the area known as **Chamberí**, which underwent development in the second half of the 19th century but still retains a *castizo* air and a family atmosphere, despite not being in the oldest part of the city.

East of Paseo de la Castellana is the stylish **Salamanca** *ensanche* (extension), constructed on a grid during the late 19th century. Its tree-lined streets play host to some of the fanciest shops in Madrid. South of this, bordering the Parque del Buen Retiro, the **Retiro** neighbourhood feels slightly less exclusive but is very pleasant, thanks to its greenery.

It's easy being green in the Parque del Buen Retiro (p19)

Itineraries

With some of the world's truly great museums (which are reason enough for coming), buildings that span the centuries, and atmospheric neighbourhoods brimming with character, Madrid has plenty of sights to keep you occupied. The sights listed here are a combination of absolute must-sees and a few lesser-known favourites. Madrid's compact nature and excellent metro system are great for visitors.

Day One

Take Madrid's pulse at **Plaza de la Puerta del Sol** (p27), then listen to its heartbeat (preferably over coffee at an outdoor table) at **Plaza Mayor** (p14). Spend at least half a day at the **Museo del Prado** (p8) before lunching at a traditional restaurant in the **Los Austrias** (p50) area – something on Calle de Cava Baja. After lunch visit the **Palacio Real** (p15). Start the night sampling some tapas before dining in **Chueca** (p54).

Day Two

Start the day with a tour of **Real Monasterio de las Descalzas Reales** (p16) before heading to the **Museo Thyssen-Bornemisza** (p10) for a few hours. Refuel in **Salamanca** (p56), then shop till you drop in the barrio before a stroll through the **Parque del Buen Retiro** (p19). Indulge in a glass of *cava* (champagne) or a cocktail at **Café del Círculo de Bellas Artes** (p61) or **Museo Chicote** (p62) before an evening stroll among the twinkling lights and grand buildings of **Gran Vía** (p18).

Day Three

Time for the **Centro de Arte Reina Sofía** (p12), followed by a trip out to **San Lorenzo de El Escorial** (p36). If it's your last evening, pull an all-nighter in either rockin' Malasaña, gay Chueca or just plain popular Huertas and Santa Ana.

Worst of Madrid

- dog poo on the streets – or your shoes
- the crowds at tourist attractions on Wednesday and Sunday (free days)
- roadworks, roadworks, roadworks
- good local bars polluted by *tragaperras* – pokie machines
- noise pollution

Stroll along Gran Vía, dodging the worst of Madrid

GUY MOBERLY

Highlights

MUSEO DEL PRADO (3, J5)

In a city with three truly great art museums, the Museo del Prado sits at the top of the heap for most visitors – indeed, the Prado is reason enough for many to come to Madrid. The building itself – completed in 1785 – served as a natural history museum and laboratories, and as a cavalry barracks before its conversion in 1819 to a repository of Spanish art held in royal collections. The collection has more than 7000 works, with less than half on display. A grand extension (which is overdue and overbudget as we write) will see space created in the Casón del Buen Retiro, the nearby Museo del Ejército and in the former cloisters of the Iglesia de San Jerónimo El Real (connected to the main building via a subterranean passage). Don't feel too dejected if you find that you don't cover everything on your first visit here – aim for a couple of visits of about fours hours' duration (each) instead!

RICHARD NEBESKY

Velázquez' guest appearance in *Las Meninas*

Highlights of the ground floor include *The Story of Nastagio degli Onesti* – a perplexing work by Sandro **Botticelli** – *The Triumph of Death* by Pieter **Brueghel** the Elder, **Titian**'s *Danaé and the Shower of Gold,* and **Tintoretto**'s *Christ Washing the Disciples' Feet.* The works of **El Greco** can be seen in Rooms 60a, 61a and 62a; of particular note are his striking *Crucifixion* and *San Andrés and San Francisco.*

On the 1st floor, unmissables abound, with non-Spanish works such as *Atalanta and Hippomenes* by Guido **Reni** (see Plaza de la Cibeles, p27), *David and Goliath* by **Caravaggio**, Orazio **Gentileschi**'s *The Finding of Moses* and **Poussin**'s *Parnassus*. However, it's the Spanish works that dominate the experience: José **de Ribera**'s sweet-eyed *Magdalen* and *Martyrdom of St Phillip* demonstrate the Spanish 17th-century talent for depicting the lives of the saints, while a magnificent collection of **Velázquez**' paintings is housed in Room 12. Take your time with his innovative depiction of *The Triumph of Bacchus,* where his brilliant technical skill meets a reworking of still-life tradition. His extraordinary works of portraiture should also be given ample time, before feasting your eyes on *Las Meninas*, perhaps the most extraordinary painting of the 17th century. It depicts Velázquez himself (on the left) painting a portrait (it is assumed) of King Felipe IV and Mariana of Austria (visible in the mirror) while the Infanta Margarita and her *meninas* (maids) enter the room, in the company of dwarves. Velázquez depicts himself with the cross of the Order of Santiago on his breast – years before it was granted to him. The mathematical composition of the

> **DON'T MISS**
> • Spain's greats – El Greco, Velázquez and Goya
> • Fra Angelico's *Annunciation* – with its original frame
> • Bosch's *Garden of Earthly Delights*
> • Rubens' *Three Graces*

painting and use of perspective is a singular achievement in Spanish painting, as is the revolutionary device of creating such a direct relationship between the painting's viewers and its subjects, all the while meditating on the act of painting.

Masterpieces by **Goya** can also be found on the 1st floor (Rooms 32 and 34 to 39). These last rooms contain his haunting *Pinturas Negras* (Black Paintings), including the truly disturbing *Saturn Devouring one of his Sons*. Also in these rooms are *The 2nd of May* and *The 3rd of May*, which portray the 1808 anti-French revolt in Madrid and it's grisly repercussions, respectively. On the 2nd floor, which devotes its southern wing to Goya, you'll find the charming *La Maja Vestida* and *La Maja Desnuda*, both portraits of the same woman (her identity is still hotly debated) – one clothed, one nude. If you continue upstairs you'll find Goya's preparatory paintings for tapestries, plus religious paintings and drawings, and works by Anton Raphael **Mengs** and **Tiepolo**.

Madrid's greatest gallery, some of Spain's greatest artists; a visit to the Prado is truly, er, great

MUSEO THYSSEN-BORNEMISZA   (3, H4)

Baron Thyssen-Bornemisza was a voracious collector of predominantly European art who was happiest when buying a painting a week. The neoclassical Palacio de Villahermosa was overhauled to house the 800-odd piece collection, and in 2000 two adjoining buildings were acquired to hold a further 300 paintings (the collection of the baron's wife Carmen), which opened in 2004. The two collections, which represent one of the greatest and most wide-ranging private collections of predominantly European art, have been cleverly integrated and are best viewed in chronological order. While perusing the art, make note of the fact that even the 'no smoking' signs are small canvases – all part of the pleasure of a visit to this beautifully presented collection.

INFORMATION
- ☎ 91 369 01 51
- 🖳 www.museothy ssen.org
- ✉ Paseo del Prado 8
- € €6/4, temporary exhibitions €6/4, combined ticket €10/6, under-12s free
- ☼ 10am-7pm Tue-Sun
- ⓘ multilingual audioguides €5
- Ⓜ Banco de España
- ♿ very good
- ✕ cafeteria/restaurant

GUY MOBERLY

Start perusing the baron's collection on the 2nd floor, where you'll find a remarkable series of medieval triptychs and paintings of Italian, German and Flemish origin; Room 3's minuscule *Our Lady of the Dry Tree* demands a closer look. Room 4 highlights 15th-century Italian art, while Hans **Holbein** the Younger's wonderful *Henry VIII* can be found in Room 5 among an assortment of early Renaissance portraiture. Room 6 hosts a sampling of Italian masters such **Raphael**, **Titian** and **Tintoretto**, and a darkly beautiful *Saint Casilda* by Francisco de **Zurbarán**. Rooms 7 to 10 are devoted to 16th-century works from Italy, Germany, and the Netherlands. Four pieces by **El Greco** are displayed in Room 11. Rooms 13 to 15 display Italian, French and Spanish works of the 17th century, followed by 18th-century Italian work in Rooms 16 to 18, with some wonderful views of Venice by **Canaletto**. **Rubens**' *The Toilet of Venus* dominates the 17th-century works of Flemish, Dutch and German origin found in Rooms 19 to 21, with Anton **van Dyck**, Jan **Brueghel** and **Rembrandt** also represented.

After this, you can start with the 2nd-floor collection of Carmen Thyssen-Bornemisza, which ranges from the 17th to the 20th centuries, but emphasises 19th-century works and Spanish, American, impressionist and expressionist art, with some excellent landscapes. Unlike the baron's collection, the rooms of which are numbered, this collection moves on alphabetical lines, starting with Room A and the 17th century (with more Brueghel and van Dyck). Room D holds some lovely 18th-century works by **Boucher** and **Fragonard**, and other rooms continue through to 19th-century American works and early impressionism (Room H).

The 1st floor continues with the 17th-century Dutch theme from Rooms 22 to 26 of the baron's collection, and some still lifes in Room 27. Room 28 gives 18th-century art a look-in with **Gainsborough**. Other artists from before the 19th century (North American and European) take over Rooms 29 to 31, with John Singer **Sargent**, John **Constable** and Gustave **Courbet**. Lovers of impressionist and postimpressionist works will be delighted by the museum's collection in Rooms 32 to 33, with paintings by **Renoir**, **Degas**, **Manet**, **Monet** and **Van Gogh**. Then, in a flurry of colour, Rooms 34 to 40 highlight fauvist and expressionist art in all their coruscating brilliance, with Egon **Schiele**, Henri **Matisse**, Edvard **Munch** and **The Blue Rider** school founded by Vasili Kandinsky. The adjacent collection of Carmen Thyssen-Bornemisza continues where it left off with impressionism and postimpression before reaching expressionism and cubism, which meets up at the original collection's expressionist works in Room 37.

> **DON'T MISS**
> - Ghirlandaio's portrait of *Giovanna Tornabuoni*
> - Caravaggio's *St Catherine of Siena*
> - Kaspar David Friedrich's *Easter Morning*
> - Gauguin's *Mata Mua*

On the ground floor, visitors get a powerful dose of the 20th century, from cubism to pop art. The experimental avant-gardes have commandeered Rooms 41 to 44, with **Picasso** and Juan **Gris** flying the Spanish flag, plus Georges **Braque**. In Room 45 European modernism prepares you for the next room's focus on works from the USA, including a stunning Mark **Rothko** and works by Georgia **O'Keeffe**. For the last two rooms, it's late-surrealism to pop art, with Edward **Hopper**'s *Hotel Room* a firm fave with the crowds. Lucien **Freud**'s wonderful *Portrait of Baron Thyssen-Bornemisza* in Room 48 gives the visitor a chance to compare the complexity of the sitter's face as depicted here with the full-length portrait of the museum's namesake hanging near the entrance.

Those who can't afford to buy a painting each week can enjoy the baron's collection instead

GUY MOBERLY

CENTRO DE ARTE REINA SOFÍA (2, C9)

The expansive Centro de Arte Reina Sofía was adapted from the remains of the 18th-century San Carlos hospital with the intention of presenting the best Madrid has to offer in 20th-century Spanish art. The occasional appearance of non-Spanish artworks provides some useful comparisons between the Iberian works and the outside world. The museum's position in bohemian Lavapiés contrasts nicely with such space-age touches as the shiny steel-and-glass external elevators and a new wing designed by architect Jean Nouvel that's taking shape behind the original structure.

INFORMATION
☎ 91 774 10 00
🖥 http://museoreina
sofia.mcu.es
✉ Calle de Santa
Isabel 52
€ €3/1.50, under-18s,
over-65s & 2.30-
9pm Sat & Sun free
🕑 10am-9pm Mon-
Sat, 10am-2.30pm
Sun
ℹ multilingual
audioguides €3
Ⓜ Atocha
♿ very good
✖ cafeteria

RICHARD NEBESKY

The gallery refers to its ground floor as the 1st floor; we'll use the gallery's floor-numbering system here. At the time of research the museum's permanent collection was displayed over the 2nd and 4th floors. The 1st and 3rd floors are used to stage some excellent temporary exhibitions.

Room 1 (2nd floor) gives visitors an introduction to Spanish painting at the turn of the 20th century, which tended to be dominated by the Barcelona scene. Among the artists featured are Santiago **Rusiñol**, Ramón **Casas**, and Isidro **Nonell**, along with the important Basque painter Ignazio **Zuloaga**.

Room 2 concentrates on Madrileño José Gutiérrez **Solana**, whose dark-hued *La Tertulia de Café de Pombo* depicts an intellectual gossip session typical of 1920s Madrid (the artist depicts himself on the far right of the painting). Room 3 presents a mix of Spanish and foreign painters whose work came before, during and after cubism, best exemplified by the works of Juan **Gris** in Room 4. Bronze and iron sculptures by Pablo **Gargallo** are on display in Room 5.

The massive Room 6 is devoted to **Picasso** and dominated by the extraordinary *Guernica*. The painting (which is the sole reason many visitors come to this museum) is surrounded by a plethora of Picasso's preparatory sketches, and was commissioned by Spain's republican government for the Paris Exposition Universelle in 1937. That was the year that the German Condor Legion (working for Nationalist forces) bombed the Basque town of Gernika (Guernica), provoking outrage in Spain and abroad. The 3.5m by 7.8m painting, which Picasso did not want in Spain during the Franco dictatorship, was only returned from the USA in 1981. The breathtaking force of the work – it is the greatest painting of the 20th

Contemplate Picasso's genius and the brutality of war through the extraordinary *Guernica*

century and one of the starkest depictions of war's brutality – is heightened by the knowledge that Picasso was able to concentrate both his fury and his skill in such a short period of time.

After such an experience, Room 7 showcases the primary-coloured works of Joan **Miró**. Those with a penchant for surrealist extravaganzas will love Room 10, with Salvador **Dalí**'s *The Great Masturbator* (1929). Rooms 11 and 12 have other surrealist works, including films by filmmaker Luis **Buñuel** (his *Perro Andaluz* is not suitable for children) while Room 13 hosts works by artists active in the turbulent 1920s and 1930s. Luis **Fernández**, Benjamin **Palencia** and sculptor Alberto **Sánchez** are represented in Rooms 14 and 15, with Joan **Miró** sculptures in Room 16.

The 4th floor comprises artworks created after the civil war – in an atmosphere of Francoist repression – through to the present day, starting with Juan Manuel Díáz **Caneja** landscapes in Room 18 and works by Madrid-born artists such as Luis **Castellano** and Ángel **Ferrant**. In Room 19, Barcelona's Antoni **Tápies**' textural explorations are worth noting. Abstract painting comes to the fore in Rooms 20 to 23, with members of the **Equipo 57** group on display. From Room 24, the 1960s and 1970s are given an airing, with foreign references pro-

DON'T MISS
- Pablo Gargallo's *Máscara de Greta Garbo con mechón*
- Dora Maar's photographs of the making of *Guernica*
- Antonio Saura's *Ginto No 7*
- Manuel Valdés' *Libros IV*

vided by Francis **Bacon** (a disturbing reclining figure), Danish artist Asger **Jørn** and Henry **Moore**. The present day, from Room 38, is given over to works by Eduardo **Arroya**, while monumental sculptures by Eduardo **Chillida** fill Rooms 42 and 43. Rooms 40 and 41 highlight recent works by artists such as Ross **Bleckner**, Donald **Judd** and Elsworth **Kelly**, with Gerhard **Richter**'s enormous *Green-Blue* lording it over Room 45.

PLAZA MAYOR   (3, D4)

The Puerta del Sol may feel like the hub of Madrid, but Madrid's imperial heart beats loudest at Plaza Mayor – the town square designed in 1619 by Juan Gómez de Mora. In the Middle Ages this area was positioned outside

the city walls and known as Plaza del Arrabal. Traders liked the location as it enabled them to peddle their wares free from intramural taxation. The *alhóndiga del pan* – where wheat and flour to make bread were sold – was located here (to be replaced by the **Real Casa de la Panadería**, or royal bakery) along with butchers' stalls, fishmongers, wine stores and more. There are still plenty of shops in the plaza, and they're often good places to pick up local craft objects.

In 1673 food vendors raised tarpaulins above their stalls, thus protecting their wares (and themselves) from the refuse that people habitually tossed out of their windows from above. A fire in 1790 destroyed much of the plaza, but with Juan de Villanueva's supervision, a more-or-less faithful reproduction was soon delivered to the people of Madrid.

In the past, the plaza was the site of royal festivities, autos-da-fé (the ritual condemnation and burning of heretics) and bullfights.

DON'T MISS
- a morning coffee at any of the cafés
- the Sunday morning stamp and coin collectors' market
- buying a lurid 'your name here' bullfighting or flamenco poster

These days it's largely given over to those fancying an alfresco drink or snack, or wanting to meet up with people in an obvious location (the sculpted horse that Felipe III sits astride is a popular choice). And if you think the murals adorning the Real Casa de la Panadería look a little modern, you're right. They're a 1990s addition, and a surprising success.

Home through the ages to bullfighters, heretics, medieval traders and stamp collectors

PALACIO REAL

(3, A3)

Madrid's *alcázar* (fortress) burned down in 1734, giving King Felipe V the chance to really make his mark in the city with a dose of architectural splendour.

Felipe didn't live long enough to see the fruits of architects Filippo Juvara and Giovanni Batista Sacchetti's labours. Construction of the Italianate baroque palace lasted 26 years, by which time King Carlos III was in charge, and much of the palace's interior reflects his predilections. There are 2800 rooms, of which you can visit around 50.

Access to the apartments is via the northern end of Plaza de la Armería, where you'll ascend the grand stairway to **Halberdier's rooms**, before entering the sumptuous blood-red and gold **Throne Room** with a

INFORMATION
- ☎ 91 454 88 00
- 🖥 www.patrimonio nacional.es
- ✉ Calle de Bailén
- € €9/3.50, under-5s & Wed for EU citizens free
- 🕑 9am-6pm Mon-Sat, to 3pm Sun & hols Apr-Sep; 9.30am-5pm Mon-Sat, to 2pm Sun & hols Oct-Mar
- Ⓜ Ópera
- ♿ good

striking Tiepolo ceiling. After this, you'll enter the **rooms of Carlos III**. His drawing room features a vault fresco, *The Apotheosis of Trajan* by Anton Raphael **Mengs**. The blue antechamber, decorated in the neoclassical style, also has ceiling work by Mengs, this time depicting the *Apotheosis of Hercules;* there are also four portraits by **Goya**.

The **Gasparini Room** features walls of embroidered chinoiserie silk and an exquisite stucco ceiling. The extraordinary **Porcelain Room** (the name says it all) has elaborate details climbing every surface. Many of the rooms are awash with a predominant colour (yellow, green, blue or red), and in the midst of such luxury comes the sumptuous **Gala Dining Room**, with seating for what seems like thousands, and some staggering examples of tapestry work.

DON'T MISS
- the Armería Real (Royal Armoury)
- the Farmacia Real (Royal Pharmacy)
- the changing of the guard (noon, first Wednesday of every month, September to June)
- the view from Plaza de la Armería to the west

Enjoying the view of the Plaza de la Armería

RICHARD NEBESKY

REAL MONASTERIO DE LAS DESCALZAS REALES

(3, D3)

The Real Monasterio de las Descalzas Reales is an oasis of calm in the heart of frenetic Madrid. This unmissable treasure trove of art exists thanks to Doña Juana of Austria, Felipe II's sister, who converted the former palace into a Franciscan convent (there are still some nuns cloistered here) in the mid-16th century. She was followed by the Descalzas Reales (Barefooted Royals), a group of illustrious women who became Franciscan nuns, bringing some extraordinary works of art with them.

RICHARD NEBESKY

INFORMATION

- ☎ 91 547 53 50
- 🖳 www.patrimonio nacional.es
- ✉ Plaza de las Descalzas 3
- € €5/2.50, under-5s & Wed for EU citizens free, combined ticket with Convento de la Encarnación (p24) €6/3.40
- 🕙 10.30am-12.45pm & 4-5.45pm Tue-Thu & Sat, 10.30am-12.45pm Fri, 11am-1.45pm Sun & hols
- ⓘ compulsory guided tour (English available) included in entry fee
- Ⓜ Sol, Callao

The convent's centre features a small garden with orange trees and a fountain, its simplicity in marked contrast to the elaborate **Renaissance stairway**, which features lavish fresco work and a painted vault by Claudio Coello. A portrait of Felipe II and three royal children looks down at visitors from the top of the stairs – with a suitably sombre and inbred cast to their features.

There are 33 (Christ's age at death) **chapels** in the convent, and a compulsory tour takes you past several of them. The first contains an eerily realistic recumbent Christ. The tombs of Doña Juana and Empress Maria of Austria are in the choir, which has 33 stalls (the convent's maximum capacity is 33 nuns). The convent also contains an extraordinary collection of 17th-century **tapestries** from Brussels, which are kept in the former sleeping quarters. Along the way, try spotting works by Rubens, Titian and Brueghel. Four or five artisans could take as long as a year to weave a square metre of premium-quality tapestry, so imagine how many years must have gone into these!

DON'T MISS

- the Bosch-style painting of the *Ship of Salvation*
- Pedro de la Mena's *Dolorosa*
- *The Triumph of the Holy Eucharist over Idolatry* – a tapestry by Rubens

PLAZA DE LA VILLA (3, B4)

It is thought that this plaza was chosen to be the city's permanent seat of government in the late Middle Ages. It's one of Madrid's most beautiful spots, with a sense of history and some damn fine architecture.

The plaza's oldest structure is the early-15th-century **Casa de los Lujanes**, which has an exquisite tower, Gothic portals and Mudéjar arches. The tower is said to have held the imprisoned French monarch François I and his sons after they were captured during the Battle of Pavia in 1525.

INFORMATION

- ⓘ free guided tours of the *ayuntamiento* (in Spanish) at 5pm & 6pm Mon (arrive 10mins before)
- Ⓜ Ópera
- ♿ limited

The **Casa de Cisneros** was constructed in 1537 by the nephew of Cardinal Cisneros, who was a key adviser to Queen Isabel. It is *plateresque* (Spanish Renaissance) in inspiration, although it was much restored and altered at the beginning of the 20th century. The most obvious signs of the Renaissance style are visible in the main door and window above. It now serves as the *alcalde* (mayor's office).

A Tight Budget

The austere demeanour of Madrid's *ayuntamiento* is due to the scarcity of funds for municipal buildings during the 17th century. As a matter of fact the *consejo* (town council) had met for the previous three centuries in the Iglesia de San Salvador (no longer standing), which once faced the plaza on Calle Mayor.

A marvellous enclosed bridge links the Casa de Cisneros building with Madrid's 17th-century **ayuntamiento** (town hall), which stands on the western side of the plaza. This building is a wonderful example of the *barroco madrileño* (Madrid baroque) style, with Herrerian slate-tile spires. It was originally planned by Juan Gómez de Mora to be a prison, but ended up serving as both a prison and a town hall.

RICHARD NEBESKY

Imagine the *ayuntamiento* they might have built if the budget hadn't been so tight...

GRAN VÍA (3, B1–G3)

Madrid's mighty boulevard cuts a southeastwards swathe through the city from Plaza de España to Calle de Alcalá. It is in parts tacky, energetic, elegant and garish. You'll find luxury hotels, *hostales* (cheap hotels), fast-food joints, sex shops, chain stores, fashion houses, Internet cafés, cinemas, theatres and nightclubs, and a whole lot of people and vehicles.

INFORMATION
Ⓜ Plaza de España,
Santo Domingo,
Callao, Gran Vía

Gran Vía was constructed in the first decades of the 20th century, when over a dozen streets were discarded and entire neighbourhoods bulldozed, all to be replaced by grand architectural piles. Spain's neutral status in WWI made Madrid a prosperous city when other European capitals were riven with poverty.

Keep your eyes peeled for some buildings of note situated along Gran Vía (it can be tricky when there's so much throbbing life at ground level!), which provide a progressive tour through the 20th century's architectural trends. At Gran Vía 1 there's the 1916 **Edificio Grassy** (look for the Piaget sign), with a circular 'temple' as its crown. At No 12 is an Art-Deco delight of a bar, the **Museo Chicote** (see p62). Gran Vía 28 is the site of Madrid's first skyscraper, the 1920s **Telefónica** building, designed by US architect Louis S Weeks, while the intersection at Plaza Callao is rich in Art Deco–era cinemas (and human traffic!). Technically on Calle de Alcalá, the **Edificio Metropolis**, designed by Jules and Raymond Février was completed in 1910 (the victory statue was only placed on top in 1975). Note the beautiful dome with gilded details. You could be forgiven for thinking you're in Paris when you catch sight of this magnificent building.

Big Guns

During the civil war, the length and breadth of Gran Vía meant it was a prime target for artillery shells thundering in from the front lines around the Ciudad Universitaria to the north. Gran Vía was subsequently nicknamed 'Howitzer Alley'. The Telefónica building was a particularly favoured target, due to its status as the city's tallest building.

Being the city's tallest building had its down side during the civil war

PARQUE DEL BUEN RETIRO (2, D8)

Madrid's magnificent green lungs began as the Real Sitio del Buen Retiro, or palatial grounds of King Felipe IV (1621–65). After Isabel II's ousting in 1868, the park was opened to one and all, which is exactly what you'll find on any weekend in this busy, vital and beautiful spot. Buskers, hawkers, potheads, families, lovers, fortune-tellers, puppeteers, cyclists, joggers, and tourists all soak up the leisure options and add to the atmosphere – particularly on a Sunday morning, or after Sunday lunch.

INFORMATION
- 6am-midnight May-Sep, 6am-10pm Oct-Apr
- **M** Retiro
- ♿ good

The artificial lake *(estanque)* is watched over by the massive structure of **Alfonso XII's mausoleum**. The western side of the lake features the **Fuente Egipcia** (Egyptian Fountain), where legend says a fortune was buried (unfortunately not true). It's possible to hire boats for a quick paddle – you'll pay around €5 for the experience.

South of the lake you'll find the **Palacio de Velázquez** and the **Palacio de Cristal** (Crystal Palace), which were both built by Ricardo Velázquez Bosco. The Palacio de Cristal, a particularly charming metal-and-glass structure, was built in 1887 as a winter garden for exotic flowers. Occasional exhibitions are held here and in the Palacio de Velázquez.

Paradise Lost
In the southern half of the park you may notice an unusual choice of subject for one of the city's statues. *El Ángel Caído* (The Fallen Angel) is a statue of none other than Lucifer.

On 11 March 2005 the city's memorial to the victims of the terrorist attacks of the year before was unveiled on the western flank of the park. Called **El Bosque de los Ausentes** (Forest of the Absent), it features a spiralling path surrounded by 191 trees and a shallow, serpentine moat.

The very southern part of the park's borders contains one of Madrid's loveliest examples of 18th-century architecture – the **Observatorio Astronómico** (Astronomical Observatory), designed by Juan de Villanueva for King Carlos III.

Come for a boat ride on the lake, or to pay your respects to Alfonso XII

RICHARD NEBESKY

EL RASTRO (3, D6)

Sunday morning may seem quiet in other parts of Madrid, but in the area around Calle de Embajadores things are positively humming by 9am, buzzing by 11am and exploding by 2pm. El Rastro flea market has been given mixed coverage for years now, with some believing it's not as good as it used to be, and that it caters mostly to tourists nowadays.

Rubbish! On any given Sunday you'll find the streets choked with Madrileños, tourists, pickpockets (watch your bags) and a cornucopia of stalls selling whatever you fancy – clothes, accessories, electrical goods, music, plants, furniture, art, food, drink and general junk.

INFORMATION

✉ from Plaza de Cascorro, down Calle Ribera de Curtidores

🕐 8am-3pm Sun & hols

Ⓜ La Latina

Disappointingly few fleas for sale

What's in a Name?

Wondering where the market gets its name from? It comes from the fact that the area was a meat market in the 17th and 18th centuries – *rastro* refers to the trail of blood left behind when animals were dragged down the hill.

The main action takes place from Plaza de Cascorro down Calle Ribera de Curtidores, although it's always worth wandering off into the sidestreets and perusing the makeshift stalls that are set up on blankets and sheets placed on the ground. The less-transient shops of the neighbourhood are also doing a roaring trade, with second-hand shops (often specialising in particular goods) staying open on what's supposed to be a day of rest. Calle de Arganzuela, for example, seems to be *the* place if you're into military antiques and old office goods. The cafés, bars and restaurants of the neighbourhood provide sustenance for those who need refuelling (some of the streets are quite steep). Places to eat generally get really crowded from 2pm – when the market is at its peak and people start to think about lunch.

Sights & Activities

MUSEUMS & GALLERIES

Casa de Lope de Vega
(3, G5) Felix Lope de Vega was one of Spain's leading golden-age writers, and he moved to this austere-looking house in 1610, remaining here until his death in 1635. You wouldn't really know he's no longer with us though, as it's filled with memorabilia pertaining to his life and times, giving a wonderful insight into life in Madrid in the 17th century.
☎ 91 429 92 16 ⊠ **Calle de Cervantes 11** € €2/1 ☽ **9.30am-2pm Tue-Fri, 10am-noon Sat** Ⓜ **Antón Martín**

Ermita de San Antonio de la Florida (2, A6) This little hermitage has two small chapels: the southern one contains a magnificent dome fresco by Goya depicting the miracle of St Anthony. The crowd of people swarming around the saint are interesting because they've been placed in the dome, an area usually reserved for heavenly subjects. The artist himself

is buried in the chapel, in front of the altar.
☎ 91 542 07 22 🖳 **www.munimadrid.es /ermita in Spanish** ⊠ **Glorieta de San Antonio de la Florida 5** € **free** ☽ **10am-2pm & 4-8pm Tue-Fri, 10am-2pm Sat, Sun & hols** Ⓜ **Príncipe Pío** ♿ **limited**

Fundación Juan March
(4, G5) Businessman Juan March established this cultural and scientific foundation in 1955, and the modern facilities house a permanent collection of contemporary Spanish art. Excellent temporary exhibitions and concerts are also held here on a regular basis.
☎ 91 435 42 40 🖳 **www .march.es in Spanish** ⊠ **Calle de Castelló 77** € **free** ☽ **11am-8pm Mon-Sat, to 3pm Sun & hols** Ⓜ **Núñez de Balboa** ♿ **limited**

Galería Moriarty (3, H1)
The Moriarty on Calle del Almirante became a central

point of artistic exuberance during *la movida* (the post-Franco cultural revolution), and is still going strong. A parade of artists marched through the gallery, among them such leading lights as Ceesepe (b 1958), whose real name is Carlos Sánchez Pérez, and Ouka Lele (b 1956).
☎ 91 531 43 65 🖳 **www.galeriamoriarty .com** ⊠ **Calle del Almirante 5** € **free** ☽ **11am-2pm & 5-8.30pm Tue-Fri, 11am-2pm Sat** Ⓜ **Chueca**

Max Estrella Art Gallery
(3, H1) With a strictly contemporary agenda, this very modern gallery plays host to talented emerging artists such as Begoña Montalbán, Paloma Navares and Javier de Juan.
☎ 91 319 55 17 🖳 **www.maxestrella.com** ⊠ **Calle de Santo Tomé 6** € **free** ☽ **11am-2pm & 4.30-8.30pm Mon-Fri, 11am-2pm & 6-9pm Sat** Ⓜ **Colón**

Discount Cards
If you intend to do some intensive sightseeing and travelling on public transport, consider the **Madrid Card** (www.madridcard.com). It includes free entry to 40 museums in and around Madrid, plus unlimited use of public transport, the Madrid Visión tourist bus, discounts in certain shops and restaurants and a free tour of Habsburg Madrid (Los Austrias) on Saturdays. The ticket is available for one/two/three days (€28/42/55). Purchase it at the tourist offices on Plaza Mayor and in Calle del Duque de Medinaceli (see p90), via the website, on the Madrid Visión bus and in some travel agents.

The Paseo del Arte ticket covers the 'big three' galleries (Museo del Prado, Museo Thyssen-Bornemisza and Centro de Arte Reina Sofía) for €7.66 and is valid for a year (one visit each). For unlimited visits to either the Prado or the Reina Sofía, a year's ticket costs €24.04. A yearly ticket to both these galleries and eight other museums throughout the country costs €36.06.

Closed, but no Cigar

Most, but not all, museums and monuments close on Monday. Just about everything is also shut on Sunday afternoon. In July and August some museums close parts of their displays for want of staff, most of whom take annual leave around this time. A few minor museums close entirely throughout August. Admission to many galleries, museums and other sights is free at least one day per week; in a few cases this is restricted to EU citizens. Young children are given free entry to most tourist sites.

Museo Arqueológico Nacional (4, E6) Founded by royal decree in 1867, this is one mother of a royal collection, with goodies from prehistory to Ancient Egypt, Greece and Rome, up to Mudéjar Spain. Among other things, keep an eye out for the sarcophagus of Amemenhat, the Lady of Elche, Recesvinio's crown and the Aljafería arch.
☎ 91 577 79 12 🖳 www .man.es in Spanish ✉ Calle Serrano 13 € €3/1.50, under-18s & over-65s 2.30-8.30pm Sat & 9.30am-2.30pm Sun free ☽ 9.30am-8.30pm Tue-Sat, to 2.30pm Sun & hols Ⓜ Colón ♿ good

Museo de América (2, A5)
When the Spaniards weren't loading their ships with Latin American gold, they found a bit of room for transporting ceramics, statuary, jewellery, hunting implements and a few shrunken heads from indigenous cultures. Some very good temporary exhibitions with Latin American themes are also held in this interesting museum.
☎ 91 549 26 41 ✉ Avenida de los Reyes Católicos 6 € €3/1.50 ☽ 9.30am-3pm Tue-Sat, 10am-3pm Sun & hols Ⓜ Moncloa ♿ good

Museo de Cerralbo (3, A1)
This is the former 19th-century home of the 17th Marqués de Cerralbo – politician, poet, archaeologist, as well as avid collector. The collection has been kept close to how the Marqués lived, and according to his wishes. It includes religious paintings (El Greco's *Éxtasis de San Francisco* is stunning), clocks, suits of armour, jewellery and books. Most of the opulent rooms are fascinating – you'll feel like a right stickybeak at times.
☎ 91 547 36 46 ✉ Calle de Ventura Rodríguez 17 € €2.40/1.20, under-18s & over-65s Wed & Sun free ☽ 9.30am-8pm Tue-Sat, 10am-3pm Sun & hols Ⓜ Plaza de España, Ventura Rodríguez

Take the kids along to Museo de San Isidro

Museo de San Isidro (3, B6) Madrid's patron saint has a museum named after him, where you can see various archaeological finds from old Madrid, including mosaic fragments from the Roman villa in Carabanchel (now a southern suburb). The building also has a 16th-century courtyard, a 17th-century chapel and reasonably interesting displays based on the history of Madrid.
☎ 91 366 74 15 🖳 www .munimadrid.es/museo sanisidro in Spanish ✉ Plaza de San Andrés 2 € free ☽ 9.30am-8pm Tue-Fri, 10am-2pm Sat, Sun & hols Ⓜ La Latina ♿ limited

Museo Lázaro Galdiano (4, F3) Don José Lázaro Galdiano (1862–1947), a successful businessman, had this Italianate mansion built in 1903. It was his home and doubled as a museum for his art collection, with delightful works by artists such as Van Eyck, Bosch, Zurbarán, Ribera, Goya, Gainsborough and Constable held here.
☎ 91 561 60 84 🖳 www .flg.es in Spanish ✉ Calle de Serrano 122 € €4/3 ☽ 10am-4.30pm Wed-Mon Ⓜ Rubén Darío, Gregorio Marañón

Museo Municipal de Arte Contemporáneo (4, A5)

Housed in the Centro Cultural de Conde Duque, this is a strong collection of modern Spanish art, mostly paintings, along with photography, sculpture and graphic arts and an engaging roster of temporary exhibits that might include installations, digital works and other new media from around the world.
☎ 91 588 59 28 💻 www .munimadrid.es/museo artecontemporaneo in Spanish ✉ Calle del Conde Duque 9 € free 🕙 10am-2pm Tue-Sat, 10.30am-2.30pm Sun & hols M Noviciado 🚹 limited

Museo Municipal de Madrid (4, C6)

A restored baroque entrance greets visitors to this museum, but the original 1673 building's chapel (best viewed from the mezzanine) is all that remains inside, dominated by a canvas of San Fernando Ante La Virgen by Luca Giordano (1634–1705). The museum aims to bring Habsburg Madrid to life, with some decent paintings (including a couple of Goyas) and a huge model of the city from 1830.
☎ 91 588 86 72 ✉ Calle de Fuencarral 78 € free 🕙 9.30am-8pm Tue-Fri, 10am-2pm Sat, Sun & hols M Tribunal 🚹 limited

Museo Nacional de Artes Decorativas (3, J3)

Spread over five floors, this museum presents a fascinating collection of glassware, ceramics, furniture, fabrics and utensils in an attractive setting, plus some well-reconstructed rooms. A particular favourite is the *alcoba*, a room used for 'conjugal unions'. Make time to look down and up at the parquetry floors and detailed ceilings – and the 5th floor's tiled 18th-century kitchen.
☎ 91 532 64 99 💻 http:// mnartesdecorativas.mcu .es/in Spanish ✉ Calle de Montalbán 12 € €2.40/ 1.20, under-18s, over-65s & Sun free 🕙 9.30am-3pm Tue-Sat, 10am-3pm Sun & hols M Banco de España, Retiro

Museo Sorolla (4, E4)

The former home of artist Joaquín Sorolla is largely as it was in 1923 (the year of his death). It holds a charming collection of his light-filled impressionist works, plus personal items. The ground floor gives a great idea of the manner in which Sorolla lived and worked, with his sun-drenched studio, while the 1st floor takes you to the gallery that houses works from the 1890s onwards.
☎ 91 310 15 84 💻 http:// museosorolla.mcu.es in Spanish ✉ Paseo del General Martínez Campos 37 € €2.40/1.20 🕙 9.30am-3pm Tue-Sat, 10am-3pm Sun & hols M Iglesia

Real Academia de Bellas Artes de San Fernando (3, F3)

This rather old-fashioned gallery was founded by King Fernando VI in the 18th century as a centre to train artists

Visit Habsburg Madrid at Museo Municipal de Madrid

and can boast that both Picasso and Dalí studied here (although neither were particularly thrilled by their time here). Spanish artists of note displayed include José de Ribera, El Greco, Alonso Cano, Bravo Murillo, Goya (including his last palette), plus more modern efforts by Gris, Chillida and Sorolla (all slim pickings though).
☎ 91 524 08 64 💻 http:// rabasf.insde.es in Spanish ✉ Calle de Alcalá 13 € €2.40/1.20 🕙 9am-7pm Tue-Fri, to 2.30pm Sat-Mon M Sevilla

Travesía Cuatro (4, C6)

A relative newcomer to Madrid's dynamic gallery scene (since 2002), this edgy space specialises in photography, video and installation work and has some intriguing temporary exhibits, plus a stellar roster of hip and talented artists, such as Amparro Garrido and Carolina Silva.
☎ 91 310 00 98 💻 www .travesiacuatro.com ✉ Travesía de San Mateo 4 € free 🕙 11am-2pm & 5-8.30pm Tue-Fri, 11am-2pm Sat M Tribunal

CHURCHES & CATHEDRALS

Basílica de Nuestra Señora del Buen Consejo (Catedral de San Isidro) (3, C5) This austere, sturdy-looking baroque basilica (designed by Pedro Sánchez) underwent a few changes from its status as the Jesuit Colegio Imperial. Originally built in the 1620s, the basilica's interior was later remodelled by Ventura Rodríguez, with a lavish altar drawing the attention of visitors. It's now home to the remains of the city's patron saint, San Isidro (in the third chapel to the left from the entrance).
☎ 91 369 20 37 ⊠ Calle de Toledo 37 € free 8am-noon & 6-8.30pm M La Latina

Basílica de San Francisco el Grande (3, A6) According to legend, St Francis himself built a chapel on the site of this basilica in 1217. The present building was completed under the watchful eye of Francesco Sabatini in 1784, after Francesco Cabezas had difficulty with the enormous expanse of the 33m-diameter dome. Upon entering you will probably be directed to a series of corridors lined with art-

works behind the church's glittering high altar. Note the lovely frescoed cupolas and chapel ceilings by Francisco Bayeu.
☎ 91 365 38 00 ⊠ Plaza de San Francisco € €3 11am-1pm & 5-7pm Tue-Sat M La Latina

Basílica de San Miguel (3, C5) This basilica stands on the site of an earlier Romanesque church. The present edifice was built between 1739 and 1745 and is an interesting example of late baroque, with statues representing the four virtues on the façade. The interior is a mix of rococo and the contemporary.
☎ 91 548 40 11 ⊠ Calle de San Justo 4 € free 11am-12.45pm & 6-8.30pm Mon-Sat M Ópera, La Latina

Catedral de Nuestra Señora de la Almudena (3, A4) Just south of the Palacio Real, Madrid's cathedral is externally grand and internally bland. It was finally completed in 1993 after a good 110 years of construction – the Spanish Civil War was a major interruption. The present place of worship may well be a

View grisly relics at Convento de la Encarnación

RICHARD NEBESKY

new building, but this site (and the areas nearby) have served a religious purpose in one way or another since the city's earliest settlement. It was here that Crown Prince Felipe married Letizia Ortiz in 2004.
☎ 91 542 22 00 ☐ www .patrimonionacional.es ⊠ Calle de Bailén € free 9am-9pm M Ópera

Convento de la Encarnación (3, B2) This enclosed Augustine convent has some decent royal portraiture (it was founded by Felipe III and Margarita of Austria in 1611). However, the real reason for visiting is the jam-packed *reliquiario* (reliquary), which has more than 700 assorted skulls and bones, bits of the True Cross and a vial of St Pantaleón's blood – which liquefies on the night of 26 July.
☎ 91 547 05 10 ☐ www .patrimonionacional.es ⊠ Plaza de la Encarnación € €3.60/2, under-5s & Wed for EU

St Valentine's Bones

Apparently, St Valentine's bones lie in one of the chapels of the **Iglesia de San Antón** (more properly known as San Antonio Abad), in Malasaña. (Several other churches around Europe also claim this honour, so tourist-puller if you're a cynic.) You can view the skull-and-crossbones arrangement at Calle de Hortaleza 65 (4, C6) between 5pm and 6.30pm.

citizens free ⊙ 10.30am-12.45pm & 4-5.45pm Tue-Thu & Sat, 10.30am-12.45pm Fri, 11am-1.45pm Sun & hols Ⓜ Ópera

Iglesia de San Andrés

(3, B6) This church suffered severe damage during the civil war, but its exterior looks as neat and shiny as a new pin now. The interior features some baroque decorative touches and a lovely dome, with sculpted plump cherubs running riot in a sea of colour.
☎ 91 365 48 71 ✉ Plaza de San Andrés € free ⊙ 9am-1pm & 6-8pm Ⓜ La Latina

Iglesia de San Ginés

(3, D3) One of Madrid's oldest churches, San Ginés has been here in some shape or form since the 14th century. There's also speculation that pre-1085, when Christians arrived in Madrid, a Mozarabic community (Christians in Muslim territory) had its parish church on the site. The dark interior is ideal for contemplation of

matters both spiritual and artistic (note the El Greco painting). The church's small dome is built on the same proportions as that of St Peter's in Rome.
☎ 91 366 48 75 ✉ Calle del Arenal 13 € free ⊙ 8.45am-1pm & 6-9pm Ⓜ Ópera, Sol

Iglesia de San Jerónimo el Real

(3, J5) This church was constructed in the 16th century and was once the nucleus of the extremely powerful Hieronymite monastery. The interior structure is a 19th-century remodelling that gives more than a nod to the Monasterio de San Juan de los Reyes in Toledo. King Alfonso XIII was married here in 1906, and King Juan Carlos I was crowned here in 1975.

> ## Blink & You'd Miss It...
> You could easily be forgiven for failing to notice the small brick structure on the corner of Calle de Fuencarral and Calle de Augusto Figueroa in Chueca (3, F1). It's Madrid's **tiniest church**, and has little more than a crucifix and diminutive altar.

When we visited it was buttressed by scaffolding.
☎ 91 421 35 78 ✉ Calle del Moreto 4 € free ⊙ 9am-1.30pm & 6-8pm Ⓜ Banco de España

Iglesia de San Nicolás de los Servitas

(3, B4) A few periods are represented in this church (which is considered the oldest surviving church in the city), from the 12th-century Mudéjar bell tower, to the church itself, which dates in part from the 15th century – note the late-Gothic interior vaulting and timber ceiling. There are 18th-century baroque touches too. The architect Juan de Herrera was buried in the crypt in 1597.
☎ 91 548 83 24 ✉ Plaza de San Nicolás 6 € free ⊙ 8am-1.30pm & 5.30-8.30pm Mon, 8-9.30am & 6.30-8.30pm Tue-Sat, 9.30am-2pm & 6.30-9pm Sun Ⓜ Ópera

Iglesia de San Pedro El Viejo

(3, B5) Those wanting to see one of the few remaining examples of Mudéjar architecture should raise their eyes to San Pedro's bell tower, which dates from the 14th century.
☎ 91 365 12 84 ✉ Costanilla de San Pedro € free Ⓜ La Latina

Grand and bland Catedral de Nuestra Señora de la Almudena

PLAZAS & PARKS

Campo del Moro (2, A7)

The exquisite Campo del Moro (Moor's Field) is where an army led by Ali ben Yusef set up camp in 1110 in the vain hope of retaking Madrid. In medieval times, the area was used for jousting, and then as a playground for royal children in the 19th century. The park opened to the public under the second republic of 1931, then closed under Franco. Note the flowerbeds and the Fuente (fountain) de las Conchas, which was designed by Ventura Rodríguez.

☎ 91 454 88 00
✉ **Paseo de la Virgen del Puerto** ☺ **10am-8pm Mon-Sat, 9am-8pm Sun, to 6pm Oct-Mar** Ⓜ **Príncipe Pío**

Casa de Campo (2, A7)

Casa de Campo is a huge expanse of scrubland spreading west of the Río Manzanares for 1740 hectares. It was in royal hunting hands until 1931, after which the second

republic made it accessible to the public. During the civil war, many of Franco's troops used the area to shell Madrid, and trenches are still scattered about. Enter via the metro or by the Teleférico de Rosales (see p32). It has swimming pools, tennis courts and a lake.

Ⓜ **Batán**

Parque del Oeste (2, A5)

Nestled between the university and Moncloa metro station, this large park is a surprisingly tranquil and beautiful place to get some green in Madrid. The park was the site of the death of many locals at the hands of Napoleon's army in 1808, and was a favoured spot for the famous writer Benito Pérez Galdós.

☺ **10am-8pm** Ⓜ **Moncloa**

Plaza de Chueca (3, G1)

This party-loving plaza (the epicentre of gay Madrid) is named after a composer of

zarzuelas (light opera) and is at its best late at night. Locals, gays, party types and anyone else hang out at the tables, benches and chairs and on the ground. It's flanked by Calle de Gravina, Calle de Augusto Figueroa, apartments and (especially in summer) more than a few banners protesting about the racket.

Ⓜ **Chueca**

Plaza de Colón (4, E6)

As an inspired memorial to Christopher Columbus and his discovery of America, this plaza makes a great transport hub. The Monumento a Colón (statue of Columbus) ain't too bad, but the big slab in the Jardines del Descubrimiento (Discovery Gardens) has a distinctly 1970s cobbled-together feel about it. Still, there's a cultural centre (Centro Cultural de la Villa, p66) underneath it all, which offers entertainment potential.

Ⓜ **Colón, Serrano**

From convent to plaza, earthy to sterile, Plaza de Santa Ana has been there, done that

Lapping it up

When Real Madrid wins a big match, the club's supporters like to commandeer the fountain at the centre of Plaza de la Cibeles (right) for their festivities. The entire plaza and surrounding streets can get packed with revellers, and the damage to the fountain and litter left behind is not a pretty sight. Occasionally, the city council intervenes and boards up the fountain if it looks like victory is looming.

RICHARD NEBESKY

Plaza de España (3, B1)
Not as grand as you'd think, given its name, but this plaza is a popular meeting spot for plenty of Madrileños and has some welcoming seats under trees for hot days. Its north side faces the bombastic Edificio de España, but its centre has a bronze statue of Miguel de Cervantes, with his famous characters Don Quixote and Sancho Panza at his feet. It was quite the construction zone when we visited.
Ⓜ Plaza de España

Plaza de la Cebada to Plaza de la Paja (3, B5–C6)
This conglomeration of tiny and attractive plazas comprises one of Madrid's best spots to socialise (especially on Sundays). Plaza de la Paja was the hub of Madrid in medieval times and has been lovingly restored, affording some attractive views of its surrounds. Other miniplazas up the hill from it are Plazas de los Carros, de Puerta de Moros and del Humilladero. Plaza de la Cebada (which is more of a street) has a market.
Ⓜ La Latina

Plaza de la Cibeles (3, H3) This glorious 1780 fountain (by Ventura Rodríguez and José Hermosilla) is one of Madrid's most recognisable monuments and depicts the Ancient Greek goddess of nature, Cybele, in a chariot drawn by two lions. The story behind this myth is as follows: Cybele had Atalanta and Hippomenes turned into lions and shackled to her chariot for having profaned her temple. Aphrodite had tricked them into this, due to her displeasure at the couple's apparent ingratitude for her good work.
Ⓜ Banco de España

Plaza de la Puerta del Sol (3, E3) This is Madrid's most central point and the psychological centre of town. Check out the small plaque on the southern side that marks km 0, the point from which distances are measured along the country's highways. A good meeting point is the bronze statue of a bear nuzzling a *madroño* (strawberry tree).
Ⓜ Sol

Plaza de Neptuno (3, H4)
Officially known as Plaza de Cánovas del Castillo, but more readily referred to as Plaza de Neptuno. The sculpture of the sea-god is, for the record, by Juan Pascal de Mena. Atlético de Madrid fans flock here when their team is victorious (see above for details of Real Madrid's fans' activities), halting traffic.
Ⓜ Banco de España

Plaza de Olavide (4, C4)
You won't find anything of historical interest here but we think it's one of the city's most pleasant afternoon-evening spots. There's a large open area, plenty of bars with outdoor seating, some pretty rose bushes, play equipment for children and an authentically local feel, with few tourists disturbing the social intercourse.
Ⓜ Bilbao, Quevado, Iglesia

Plaza de Oriente (3, B3)
Between the Palacio Real and the Teatro Real is one of Madrid's loveliest plazas, which gets its French feel from Joseph Bonaparte's rule in the early 1800s. It contains an equestrian statue of Felipe IV and statues of ancient monarchs that were supposed to adorn the Palacio Real but were deemed too heavy.
Ⓜ Ópera

You'll have a real good time exploring the natural splendour of the Real Jardín Botánico

Plaza de Santa Ana
(3, F4) You can thank Joseph Bonaparte for this square; he demolished the 16th-century Convent of Santa Ana to make room for it. A long-famous drinking haunt, it was tarted up in the new millennium and many feel it has lost its earthy charm and now has an antiseptic feel. Still, it's buzzing every afternoon and night of the week, and there's even play equipment for the kids.
Ⓜ **Sevilla, Antón Martín**

Plaza del Dos de Mayo
(4, B6) This square gets its name from the heroic last stand that Madrileños took against Napoleon's troops on 2 May 1808. All that's left of the barracks that were here at the time is an arch. In more recent times, the plaza has had a reputation as the party spot for underage drinkers, although legislation has curbed the booze-and-hormone explosion to some extent.
Ⓜ **Noviciado, Tribunal**

Real Jardín Botánico
(3, J6) In 1774 King Carlos III decided that the garden sited on the banks of the Río Manzanares should be moved to Paseo del Prado, which was completed in 1781. The **Pabellón Villanueva**, a pavilion designed by Juan de Villanueva, was constructed and botany classes were taught here in the early 19th century. Today it is used to display free art exhibitions. After generations of serious neglect, the gardens were closed to the public in 1974, and seven years' of renovations carried out – well worth the effort.
☎ 91 420 30 17 ⌨ www .rjb.csic.es ✉ Plaza de Murillo 2 € €2/1 ⏱ 10am-6pm Nov-Feb, to 7pm Mar & Oct, to 8pm Apr & Sep, to 9pm May-Aug Ⓜ Atocha ♿ good

NOTABLE BUILDINGS & MONUMENTS

Biblioteca Nacional & Museo del Libro (4, E6)
The Biblioteca Nacional was commissioned in 1865 by Isabel II and completed in 1892. Inside you'll find some cleverly arranged collections on the history of writing and the gathering of knowledge. The museo is bibliophile heaven – with Arabic texts, illuminated manuscripts, and centuries-old Torahs, but it is closed until the end of 2005.
☎ 91 580 78 00 ⌨ www .bne.es ✉ Paseo de Recoletos 20 € free ⏱ 9am-9pm Mon-Fri, to 2pm Sat Ⓜ Colón ♿ good

Edificio de España
(3, B1) For some strange reason, this building, which towers over the Plaza de España, is not as hideous as you would expect fascist-era architecture to be. The building was constructed between 1947 and 1953, which was a time when Spain was not on the friendliest of terms with the rest of the world. Needless to say, it became a symbol of the 'we don't need them' school of thought for the

Franco era. It looks best at sunset.

Ⓜ **Plaza de España**

Faro de Madrid (2, A5) It may look like an air traffic control tower, but the faro (literally, 'lighthouse') exists just to provide a panoramic view of Madrid from 92m up. The views are good, though the tower's lacking in the usual touristy facilities (no café or restaurant). Look southeast towards the city centre and you'll see the Arco de la Victoria – the archway built to celebrate Franco's victory in the civil war.

☎ 91 544 81 04
✉ **Avenida de los Reyes Catolicos** € €1/50c
🕑 10am-2pm & 5-9pm Tue-Sun Ⓜ Moncloa
♿ good

Muralla Árabe (3, A4)
This is a fragment of the city wall built by Madrid's early medieval Muslim rulers. The earliest sections date from the 9th century, while others date from the 12th and 13th centuries. The council organises open-air theatre and music performances here during summer.

✉ **Cuesta de la Vega**
Ⓜ Ópera

Palacio de Comunicaciones (3, J3)
This must be one of the most elaborate post offices in the world, and the word 'palace' is not misplaced. Some find it much too grandiose, while others enjoy the sense of occasion that comes with buying a stamp. It was built in 1904 by Antonio

Palacios Ramilo in the North American monumental style, and has Gothic and Renaissance touches. At the time of writing plans were afoot to turn it into the town hall and move post office services nearby.

☎ 91 396 24 43
✉ **Plaza de la Cibeles**
🕑 8.30am-9.30pm Mon-Sat Ⓜ **Banco de España**

Plaza de Toros Monumental de Las Ventas (2, F6) This is the biggest and most important bullring in the world, and it's suitably impressive in appearance. Built in 1929 in the neo-Mudéjar style and featuring some lovely tilework, it has the capacity

to hold more than 20,000 spectators. It's worth a visit, even if you're not seeing a bullfight.

☎ 91 725 18 57
🖳 www.las-ventas.com in Spanish ✉ **Calle de Alcalá 237** Ⓜ **Las Ventas**

Puente de Segovia (2, A8) This fine nine-arched stone bridge was constructed in 1584 by Juan de Herrera for Felipe II, as a means of making San Lorenzo de El Escorial (p36) more accessible. It runs from Calle de Segovia, heading west, and is worth crossing, though the river beneath (Río Manzanares) isn't much chop.

Ⓜ **Puerta del Ángel**

Beware of levitating bulls and matadors at Plaza de Toros

A night in the sumptous Teatro Real is a gilt-y pleasure

Sociedad General de Autores y Editores

(4, D6) You'll have to admire this modernist architectural confection from the outside, which is no trouble, as it resembles a half-melted ice-cream cake and is hard to miss. It was designed by José Grasés Riera in 1902 for the banker Javier González Longoria. As a general rule you may only visit the interior on the first Monday of October, which is International Architecture Day.
☎ 91 349 95 50
✉ cnr Calles de Pelayo & de Fernando VI
Ⓜ Alonso Martínez

Teatro Real (3, B3)

Reopened in 1987, this theatre is an opulent mix of state-of-the-art theatre technology and Palacio Real–style grandeur (although some sections are reminiscent of grand-but-bland hotel lobbies).

A guided tour (in Spanish, approximately one hour) of the Teatro Real is nifty for those who want a peek inside without seeing a performance. Those who do should see p66 for details.
☎ 91 516 06 96
🖥 www.teatro-real.com in Spanish ✉ Plaza de Oriente € guided tour €4/2 🕙 guided tour every 30 mins 10.30am-1pm Mon & Wed-Fri, 11am-1.30pm Sat & Sun Ⓜ Ópera 🚹 very good

Templo de Debod (2, A7)

The Templo de Debod is something of an attention-catcher, not only for its prime position in the Parque de la Montaña, but also for the fact that it's a 2200-year-old Egyptian temple, gratefully transported to Spain in 1968 as a gesture of Egyptian thanks for Spain's help in building the Aswan High Dam.
☎ 91 366 74 15
✉ Paseo del Pintor Rosales € free 🕙 10am-2pm & 6-8pm Tue-Fri, 10am-2pm Sat & Sun Apr-Sep, 9.45am-1.45pm & 4.15-6.15pm Tue-Fri, 10am-2pm Sat & Sun Oct-Mar Ⓜ Plaza de España, Ventura Rodríguez 🚹 limited

Torres Puerta de Europa

(2, D2) These leaning office towers were a remarkable addition to Paseo de la Castellana, mostly because they stand 115m high and have a 15-degree tilt. Designed by John Burgee to symbolise a gateway to Europe, they are probably the most impressive modern structures in Madrid. Film buffs will remember them from the closing scenes of *Abre Los Ojos (Open Your Eyes)*.
✉ Plaza de Castilla
Ⓜ Plaza de Castilla

QUIRKY MADRID

Chocolatería de San Ginés (3, D3)
You may not think that a shop specialising in *churros y chocolate* (doughnuts and hot chocolate) sounds very quirky, but just look at the opening hours. This place is an early-morning rite of passage for clubbers with a dance-induced hunger.
☎ 91 365 65 46
✉ Pasadizo de San Ginés
🕙 6pm-7am Ⓜ Ópera

Hammam Medina Mayrit (3, D5)
Remember – Madrid was once Mayrit, and under Islamic rule, so pay homage to the past with a soak (reservations and swimsuits essential), massage and some tea in utterly beautiful surrounds. There's also a great Middle Eastern restaurant on the premises.
☎ 91 429 90 20
🖳 www.medinamayrit .com ✉ Calle de Atocha 14
€ hammam from €14
🕙 10am-midnight
Ⓜ Sol

Museo al Aire Libre de la Castellana (4, E4)
A space you might stumble upon and one that's often ignored by residents of Madrid, this open-air museum lies under the bridge connecting Paseo de Eduardo Dato and Calle de Juan Bravo. There are sculptures from prominent 20th-century Spanish artists (including Miró, Sánchez and Chillida) that enliven a space that's normally little more than an eyesore in most cities. All but one are on the eastern side of Paseo de la Castellana.
🖳 www.munimadrid.es /museoairelibre in Spanish
✉ Paseo de la Castellana 41 Ⓜ Rubén Darío

Museo Naval (3, H3)
This museo is a sea-dog's paradise in landlocked Madrid, and boasts dazzlingly well-crafted models of ships that'll have you itching to get out the hobby glue. Also worth noting is Juan de la Cosa's surprisingly accurate parchment map (dating from 1500) of the 'known world', and the beautiful reproduction of the Sala del Patronato.
☎ 91 379 52 99
✉ Paseo del Prado 5
€ free 🕙 10.30am-2pm Tue-Sun Ⓜ Banco de España

Museo Taurino (2, F6)
On the right-hand side of Las Ventas, this place is steeped in bull. It's small and modern, with displays

Have some good clean fun at Hammam Medina Mayrit

(English- and Spanish-language) devoted to the art-sport of man fighting bull. You'll see busts and paintings of famous bullfighters, the bloody suit worn by Manolete when he was killed by 'Islero' in 1947, and enormous bulls' heads mounted on the wall.
☎ 91 725 18 57
✉ Plaza de Toros Monumental de las Ventas
€ free 🕙 9.30am-2.30pm Mon-Sat, 10am-1pm bullfight days
Ⓜ Las Ventas

Real Madrid (2, D3)
A powerhouse of Spanish, European and international football, Real Madrid was named Team of the Century in 1998 by FIFA, and the club's list of achievements is long and impressive. While a tour of the stadium and visit to the Exposición de Trofeos (Trophy Exhibition) is a poor second to catching a match against arch rivals FC Barcelona, it's much easier to organise. You'll see the silverware and some boots of note, plus a video presentation of the club's glorious victories.
☎ 91 398 43 00
🖳 www.realmadrid .com ✉ Paseo de la Castellana 144 € tour adult/child under 14 €9/7, guided tour €14/10, Exposición de Trofeos €7/5 🕙 10.30am-6.30pm daily, only Exposición de Trofeos on match days, from 5hr before kick-off, & day after matches
Ⓜ Santiago Bernabéu

MADRID FOR CHILDREN

There's plenty to keep the littlies occupied in Madrid, from performance artists and buskers in the metro, plazas, parks and streets to attractions aimed at kids. Locals don't ascribe to the 'children should be seen and not heard' philosophy, and you'll find kids taking part in plenty of late-night dinners surrounded by grown-ups, without a whiff of condescension or irritation. Look for the 🧒 with individual reviews in the Eating, Entertainment and Sleeping chapters for more child-friendly options.

Museo de Cera (4, E6) If guffawing at waxen copies of the rich, famous and infamous is your thing, then this is your place. Adults will need to use their imagination for some of the depictions, but kids are happy to wax lyrical about the pseudo celebs and ride the Tren de Terror.
☎ 91 319 26 49
✉ Paseo de Recoletos 41
€ full visit €12/8, museo only €10/7 🕐 10am-2.30pm & 4.30-8.30pm Mon-Fri, 10am-8.30pm Sat & Sun Ⓜ Colón

Museo del Ferrocarril (2, C9) You'll find around 30 pieces of rolling stock here in the disused 1880s Estación de Delicias, about 500m south of Atocha station. Adults will enjoy the café in the 1930s dining car, and kids will love everything, especially the chance to plead for train-related toys from the shop.
☎ 902 22 88 22 🖥 www.museodelferrocarril.org
✉ Paseo de las Delicias 61
€ €3.50/2, Sat free
🕐 10am-3pm Tue-Sun
Ⓜ Delicias

Museo Nacional de Ciencias Naturales (4, E2) Kids and adults alike will love this place! Fascinating exhibitions cover topics as cool as the history of

the earth and all natural sciences, plus there's kids' programmes on weekends.
☎ 91 411 13 28
🖥 www.mncn.csic.es
✉ Calle de José Abascal 2
€ €3/2.40 🕐 10am-6pm Tue-Fri, to 8pm Sat, to 2.30pm Sun & hols, Ⓜ Gregorio Marañón, Nuevos Ministerios

Parque de Atracciones (2, A7) This is a monster-sized theme park with rides and lots of other diversions, plus some noisy, colourful summer shows. There's also the tamer Zona de Tranquilidad with a Ferris wheel.
☎ 91 463 29 00 🖥 www.parquedeatracciones.es in Spanish ✉ Casa de Campo € from €5.90, all-rides stamp €22.60/12.70
🕐 from noon Ⓜ Batán
♿ good

Teleférico de Rosales (2, A6) This cable car isn't terribly exciting, but it is an

interesting way to enter the Casa de Campo, and is never more than 40m high. Why not have lunch or a drink at one of the *terrazas* along Paseo del Pintor Rosales?
☎ 91 541 74 50 🖥 www.teleferico.com in Spanish ✉ cnr Paseo del Pintor Rosales & Calle del Marqués de Urquijo € one way/return €3.10/4.45
🕐 noon-7.30pm Sat & Sun Ⓜ Argüelles

Zoo Aquarium de Madrid (2, A7) A good zoo with more than 3000 animals (even koalas) and an aquarium with a better-than-average dolphin and sea lion show. The 3000-sq-metre aviary houses some 60 species of eagles, condors and vultures.
☎ 91 512 37 80 🖥 www.zoomadrid.com ✉ Casa de Campo € €13.50/11, under-3s free 🕐 11am-6pm Mon-Fri, 10.30am-6pm Sat, Sun & hols Ⓜ Batán ♿ good

> ## Babysitting & Childcare
> Larger hotels (especially deluxe and top-end ones) will often have an in-house babysitting service, and even medium-sized places will have a reliable contact for such things, starting at about €15 an hour and available at your hotel room. There are also numerous advertisements for multilingual babysitters in the English-language *In Madrid* publication.

Out & About

WALKING TOURS
Los Austrias Stroll

From grand 17th-century **Plaza Mayor** (**1**; p14), exit at the northwest corner and head left down Calle Mayor to historic **Plaza de la Villa** (**2**; p17), home to Madrid's 17th-century *barroco madrileño* (Madrid baroque) **ayuntamiento** (town hall; **3**) and Gothic-Mudéjar **Casa de Los Lujanes** (**4**), one of the city's oldest surviving buildings.

Follow the cobbled Calle del Cordón to Calle de Segovia, where almost in front of you is the 15th-century **Iglesia de San Pedro El Viejo** (**5**; p25), with its Mudéjar tower. Walk down Costanilla de San Pedro to nicely restored **Plaza de San Andrés** (**6**), which is the site of the **Iglesia de San Andrés** (**7**; p25). In nearby **Plaza de la Paja** (**8**), relax with a drink and snack, or take refreshments at any one of the tapas bars or traditional restaurants on **Calle de la Cava Baja** (**9**), an atmospheric old street that follows the line of the city's former 12th-century wall, before venturing down to **Basilica de San Francisco el Grande** (**10**; p24) and then strolling along Calle de Bailén to the grand **Palacio Real** (**11**; p15) and charming **Plaza de Oriente** (**12**; p27).

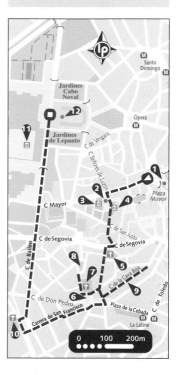

distance 2.5km
duration 2½-3hr
▶ **start** Plaza Mayor Ⓜ Sol
● **end** Plaza de Oriente Ⓜ Ópera

Travellers get ready to head off from Plaza Mayor on their walking tour

GUY MOBERLY

Paseo del Prado Parade

Start at **Plaza de la Cibeles** (**1**; p27), which separates Paseo del Prado from Paseo de los Recoletos and is encircled by some of the city's grandest buildings, including the **Palacio de Comunicaciones** (**2**; p29) – Madrid's impressive post office. Head south on the left-hand side before turning left at Calle de Montalbán, where you'll find the **Museo Nacional de Artes Decorativas** (**3**; p23), former home of

It's a jungle out there: Real Jardín Botánico

> **distance** 1km
> **duration** 1½-2hr
> ▶ **start** Plaza de la Cibeles
> Ⓜ Banco de España
> ◉ **end** Real Jardín Botánico
> Ⓜ Atocha

the Duchess of Santoña. Head back to Paseo del Prado, continuing south to Plaza de la Lealtad, where more grand architecture awaits, with the city's *bolsa* (stock exchange) and the plush **Hotel Ritz** (**4**; p70), a heady example of early-20th-century style. A little further down, you come across the **Plaza de Neptuno** (**5**; p27; so-named for its statue of the mythological sea king), which is bordered by the **Museo Thyssen-Bornemisza** (**6**; p10) as well as the mammoth **Westin Palace** (**7**; p70), which was built for the wedding of Alfonso XIII. From the plaza, you're within striking distance of the **Museo del Prado** (**8**; p8), with the **Real Jardín Botánico** (**9**) just across Plaza de Murillo, at the Prado's southern end.

Malasaña Meander

Start this walk at the gates to the **Palacio de Liria** (**1**), a glorious 1780 palace that's still in the hands of the nobility. From here, walk up Calle de Conde Duque, dominated by the enormous Centro Cultural Conde Duque, which houses the **Museo Municipal de Arte Contemporáneo** (**2**; p23). Turn right at Plaza Guardia de Corps, into Calle Cristo, before turning left at Calle Bernardo López García. This

Choice Malasaña tilework

will take you to **Plaza de las Comendadores** (**3**; p47), which has a cool Saturday afternoon market, a nice terrace atmosphere in summer and the fine 17th-century Iglesia de las Comendadores de Santiago. From here, walk along Calle de Quiñones, turn left at Calle de San Bernardo and continue to Glorieta de Ruiz Jiménez, where you walk east to Glorieta de Bilbao. Pop into the **Café Comercial** (**4**; p55) to wet the whistle. That done, head down Calle de Manuela Malasaña, named after the local 19th-century seamstress who was a heroine of the city's brief 1808 anti-French uprising. Turn left at Calle de San Andrés, where you'll find some choice tilework, the best of which can be seen in the lively depictions of pharmaceutical cures at the corner of Calle de San Vicente Ferrer. Hang a right at this last street and continue down Calle del Dos de Mayo to **Plaza del Dos de Mayo** (**5**; p28), the scene of fighting between angry Madrileños and Joseph Bonaparte's troops on 2 May 1808 and the subject of one of Goya's most famous paintings.

distance 1.75km
duration 2hr
▶ **start** Palacio de Liria
Ⓜ Ventura Rodríguez
● **end** Plaza del Dos de Mayo
Ⓜ Tribunal

DAY TRIPS
San Lorenzo de El Escorial (1, A3)

Sheltering against the protective wall of the Sierra de Guadarrama and enjoying a healthy climate, the magnificent palace-monastery complex of San Lorenzo de El Escorial is a must-see. Felipe II had the complex built in the latter half of the 16th century, consisting of a huge monastery, royal palace and mausoleum (for his parents Carlos I and Isabel), all under the watchful eye of architect Juan de Herrera.

> **INFORMATION**
> *50km northwest of Madrid*
> 🚉 line C-8a from Atocha to El Escorial (one way €2.55, 70mins, up to every 30mins), then 🚌 L1 (Circular) to San Lorenzo (€1.10, 5mins)
> 🚌 661 (one way €3, 1hr, every 20mins or so from Moncloa)
> ☎ 91 890 59 02
> 🖳 www.patrimonionacional.es
> € €7/3.50
> 🕑 10am-6pm Tue-Sun Apr-Sep, 10am-5pm Tue-Sun Oct-Mar
> ℹ guided tour €8, tourist office (☎ 91 890 53 13; Calle de Grimaldi 2; 🕑 10am-6pm Mon-Thu, 10am-7pm Fri-Sun)

The main entrance lies on the west side. Above the gateway, a statue of San Lorenzo stands watch. Enter the Patio de los Reyes, which houses statues of the six kings of Judah. Directly ahead lies the sombre basilica with its dark interior and wonderful statue of a crucified Christ, by Benvenuto Cellini.

Now go back through the patio, turn right and follow the signs to the monastery and palace quarters. There are several rooms containing tapestries, one of which has El Greco's depiction of the martyrdom of San Mauricio. You'll soon reach the stupendous Hall of Battles, a long room with extraordinary depictions of military events running its length and a beautiful barrel-vaulted ceiling painted in 1584. After this, go to the Palacio de los Austrias where you'll be able to imagine how Felipe II and his children lived. You then descend into the Panteón de los Reyes, where almost all of Spain's monarchs have been interred with their spouses. In the southeastern corner of the complex, the chapterhouses contain a minor treasure-trove of works by El Greco, Titian, Tintoretto and Bosch.

Let your thoughts take wing as you gaze at San Lorenzo de El Escorial's ceiling frescos

Toledo (1, A4)

Once set to become the capital of a united Spain, Toledo is a remarkably beautiful city, and *the* place to come for architectural history. With evidence of the Jewish, Muslim and Christian presence (all of whom lived in relative harmony), and such a concentration of Spain's artistic legacy, Toledo really does knock your socks off.

The city is built on a hill around which the Río Tajo flows on three sides. Modern suburbs spread beyond the river and walls of the *casco antiguo* (old town). Sooner or later, you'll end up at Plaza de Zocodover, the main square of the old town, from where a medieval labyrinth of streets spreads out in a confusing manner.

Just south of the plaza is the *alcázar* (closed for renovations until at least 2007) – originally a Muslim fortress in the 10th century, and later rebuilt as a royal residence for Carlos I. Just outside what were once the Arab walls, you'll find the **Museo de Santa Cruz** (☎ 92 522 10 36; Calle de Cervantes 3; admission free; ☙ 10am-2pm), a 16th-century former hospital that holds several El Greco paintings. And if that whets your appetite, you should head to Toledo's stunning **cathedral** (☎ 92 522 22 41; Calle de Cardenal Cisneros; admission €4.95; ☙ 10.30am-6.30pm Mon-Sat, 2-6pm Sun) an essentially Gothic structure that (in the 13th century) replaced the central mosque. Inside you'll find the Capilla de la Torre and the sacristy, where another collection of El Greco's works exists. El Greco's undisputed masterpiece, *The Burial of the Count of Orgaz,* can be seen in **Iglesia de Santo Tomé** (☎ 92 525 60 98; Plaza del Conde; admission €1.50; ☙ 10am-5.45pm).

INFORMATION
70km south of Madrid
- 🚊 Chamartín or Atocha stations (one way €5.15, at least 8 daily)
- 🚌 Galiano Continental buses from Estación Sur (one way €4, 50mins, every hour or so from 6.30am-10pm)
- ⓘ tourist office (☎ 92 523 40 30; Plaza del Ayuntamineto 1; ☙ 10.30am-2.30pm daily, 4.30-7pm Tue-Sun)

Holy Toledo! Check out the *alcázar* and Plaza Zocodover

DONALD & PRISCILLA EASTMAN

ORGANISED TOURS

The Patronato Municipal de Turismo organises myriad walks around Madrid. You can get information about them from any Caja de Madrid bank and its office at Plaza Mayor 3 (see p90), as well as information about other organised tours throughout the city. Keep your eyes peeled for privately run tours and the services of guides in the local press. Tours generally depart from the Plaza Mayor tourist office and cost €3.10 per adult. Some tours are conducted by bike or bus. Themes range from 'Goya in Madrid' to 'Pure and Mixed Madrid'. See www.descubremadrid .com for more details.

Adventurous Appetites (3, E3) Whet your appetite for both Madrid's historic quarter and its range of tapas bars with these informative tours that are an excellent way to make the city's acquaintance. Guides Will and James speak a number of languages each and share a wealth of knowledge about Madrid. Book in advance – tours depart from the bear statue in Plaza de la Puerta del Sol at 8pm.
☎ 639 331 073
💻 www.adventurous appetites.com € around €40 (extra for tapas & drinks)

Madrid Bike Tours Fancy a bike tour of Madrid, or further afield? This well-regarded operation can

Get a vision of Madrid on Madrid Vision

help you out. Sightseeing tours of Madrid cost €55 and feature no more than six cyclists.
☎ 680 581 782
💻 www.madridbike tours.com € from €43

Madrid Vision Backed by the *ayuntamiento,* these red double-decker buses show visitors the sights. There are three routes, frequent stops and you can buy tickets on board.
☎ 91 779 18 88
€ €13/7 ⏰ 9.30am-midnight 21 Jun–20 Sep, 10am-7pm 21 Dec–20 Mar, 10am-9pm rest of year

Paseo por el Madrid de los Austrias (3, D4) This handy tour (in Spanish and English) is organised by the *patronato,* and is a great introduction to Habsburg Madrid's sights. Buy tickets 30 minutes before the tour departs.
☎ 91 588 16 36
✉ Plaza Mayor 3
€ €3.10 ⏰ 10am or 4pm, days vary

Paseo por el Madrid del Capitán Alatriste (3, D4) Fans of sword-wielding 17th-century literary hero

Capitán Alatriste will enjoy discovering his haunts. This tour, run by the *patronato,* is conducted in English and Spanish. Buy tickets 30 minutes beforehand.
☎ 91 588 16 36
✉ Plaza Mayor 3
€ €3.10 ⏰ varies, ask at tourist office

Paseo por el Parque del Buen Retiro (2, D7) This is a good group stroll through Madrid's green lung. There's commentary in English and Spanish, and it's all under the aegis of the *patronato*. Buy tickets 30 minutes before from Caja de Madrid or information offices.
☎ 91 588 16 36
✉ Puerta del Alcalá entrance of Parque el Buen Retiro € €3.10 ⏰ varies, ask at tourist office

Pullmantur (3, B3) Offers mainstream tours, with daytime jaunts, night tours and dinner-and-show trips, as well as excursions further afield; they can also organise a bullfight visit for you.
☎ 91 541 18 07
💻 www.pullmantur -spain.com ✉ Plaza de Oriente 8 € from €19

RICHARD NEBESKY

Shopping

Madrid's shopping, whether you intended to indulge or not, will compete with many of the city's famous sites for your attention. From small local-craft shops and slick modernist fashion temples to old-fashioned food stores and full-to-bursting department stores and malls, Madrid will impress you with the quality of goods on offer, the generally reasonable prices and the courteous service. Prepare to stretch your credit card and those airline baggage restrictions to the limit!

Chueca is an excellent shopping precinct and full of fashionable shops. **Salamanca** is like Chueca's grown-up sister, with more expensive and conservative (yet still chic) tastes catered for, especially on Calle de Serrano.

If you are on the lookout for gifts and items typical of Madrid, the shops around **Plaza Mayor** and **Plaza de la Puerta del Sol** have some colourful window displays and a wealth of goodies. And of course, there's always the famous **El Rastro** to explore.

Opening Times

Most shops are open Monday to Saturday 10am to 2pm and 5pm to 8pm, although many businesses only open for the morning on Saturday. Traditional shops almost always observe the siesta, while modern ones and those on main shopping streets stay open all day. Almost all shops are closed on Sunday, unless they sell items of 'cultural significance', such as books. Some stores in the city centre operate on a rotating system of Sundays, with times signposted in the window.

RICHARD NEBESKY

CLOTHING & SHOE SIZES

Women's Clothing

Aust/UK	8	10	12	14	16	18
Europe	36	38	40	42	44	46
Japan	5	7	9	11	13	15
USA	6	8	10	12	14	16

Women's Shoes

Aust/USA	5	6	7	8	9	10
Europe	35	36	37	38	39	40
France only	35	36	38	39	40	42
Japan	22	23	24	25	26	27
UK	3½	4½	5½	6½	7½	8½

Men's Clothing

Aust	92	96	100	104	108	112
Europe	46	48	50	52	54	56

Japan	S	M	M		L	
UK/USA	35	36	37	38	39	40

Men's Shirts (Collar Sizes)

Aust/Japan	38	39	40	41	42	43
Europe	38	39	40	41	42	43
UK/USA	15	15½	16	16½	17	17½

Men's Shoes

Aust/UK	7	8	9	10	11	12
Europe	41	42	43	44½	46	47
Japan	26	27	27.5	28	29	30
USA	7½	8½	9½	10½	11½	12½

Measurements approximate only; try before you buy.

ANTIQUES & CRAFTS

Antigüedades Hom
(4, C4) Specialising in antique Spanish fans, this tiny shop is a wonderful place to browse or to find a special gift. Delicately painted fans and fans made of bone are among the items on offer. It opens afternoons only, as the owner spends the morning restoring the fans.
☎ 91 594 20 17 ✉ Calle de Juan de Austria 31 ⏱ 5.30-8.30pm Mon-Fri Ⓜ Iglesia

Casa Jiménez (3, C2)
It's easy to fall under the spell of Madrid's beautiful embroidered *mantones* (shawls), and even easier to succumb if you wander into this shop, which specialises in both *mantones* and lace wraps.
☎ 91 548 05 26 ✉ Calle de Preciados 42 ⏱ 10am-2pm & 5-8pm Mon-Sat Ⓜ Sol, Callao, Santo Domingo

Centro Puerta de Toledo
(2, B9) This large, rather soulless-looking centre has one big thing going for it – convenience. Multiple floors of art and antique dealers can be found here, plus other shops such as

A homeless Lladró figurine

wine merchants and a few fashion outlets. Mostly though, it attracts people looking for lost treasures in the form of antique furniture.
☎ 91 366 72 00 ✉ Ronda de Toledo 1 ⏱ 10.30am-9pm Tue-Sat, to 2.30pm Sun Ⓜ Puerta de Toledo

Galerías Piquer (2, B8)
If you'd like to do the bulk of your antique shopping under one roof, this centre is a good start. There are about 70 antique shops here, of varying quality and scope, but all handy to El Rastro on Sunday. Hours

may differ from shop to shop, with some closing for August.
✉ cnr Calles Ribera de Curtidores & de Rodas ⏱ 10.30am-2pm & 5-8pm Mon-Fri, 10.30am-2pm Sat & Sun Ⓜ Puerta de Toledo

Lladró (4, F5)
That much sought-after and coveted Lladró figurine your mum's been waiting for can be found here. A veritable menagerie of lonely shepherds, imploring children and beatific virgins awaits placement in the *objets d'art* cabinet.
☎ 91 435 51 12 ✉ Calle de Serrano 68 ⏱ 10am-8pm Mon-Sat Ⓜ Serrano

Luis Morueco (3, F4)
Walking through this elegant shop, which specialises in antique Spanish furniture, is like taking a tour of the wealthy Spanish homes of past centuries. Furniture, chandeliers, porcelain and paintings (most anonymous) are gracefully displayed.
☎ 91 429 57 57 ✉ Calle del Prado 16 ⏱ 9.30am-1.30pm Mon-Fri Ⓜ Antón Martín

VAT Refund
Value-added tax (VAT) is known as IVA in Spain. On accommodation and restaurant prices, it's 7% (usually included in prices). On retail goods it's 16%, and you're entitled to a refund of the 16% IVA on purchases from the one retailer totalling more than €90.15, if you take the goods out of the EU within three months. Ask for a cashback form when you make a purchase, show your passport and then present the form at the customs booth for IVA refunds when you depart Spain. You'll need your passport and proof that you're leaving the EU.

BOOKS

Berkana (3, F1) With a very strong selection of gay literature, gifts and DVDs, Berkana is a must-visit, with lots of good information about Madrid's gay scene available.
☎ 91 522 55 99
✉ Calle de Hortaleza 64
⏱ 10.30am-9pm Mon-Fri, 11.30am-9pm Sat, noon-2pm & 5-9pm Sun
Ⓜ Chueca

FNAC (3, D2) This large store not only stocks a very solid range of Spanish-language books of all descriptions, but also has French- and English-language publications, a wealth of CDs and DVDs and concert/event tickets. Madness on weekend afternoons.
☎ 91 595 61 00
✉ Calle de Preciados 28
⏱ 10am-9.30pm Mon-Sat, noon-9.30pm Sun
Ⓜ Callao

La Casa del Libro (3, E2) Madrid's leading bookshop stocks a wide selection of books on all manner of sub-jects, with some in French, some in English, and plenty in Spanish.
☎ 91 524 19 00 ✉ Gran Vía 29 ⏱ 9.30am-9.30pm Mon-Sat, 11am-9pm Sun Ⓜ Gran Vía

Panta Rhei (4, D6) This friendly bookshop has a plethora of tomes specialising in art, design, illustration and photography — and they look good enough to eat. You can also view well-selected graphics exhibitions in the edgy gallery.
☎ 91 319 89 02 ✉ Calle de Pelayo 68 ⏱ 10.30am-9pm Mon-Fri, 11am-8pm Sat Ⓜ Chueca

Petra's International Bookshop (3, C2) If you're after second-hand books that you won't mind disposing of or that you might like to add to your collection, the International Bookshop has loads, in a number of languages. Ask about the expat community chat groups if you're missing your mother tongue.
☎ 91 541 72 91 ✉ Calle de Campomanes 13 ⏱ 11am-9pm Mon-Sat Ⓜ Santo Domingo, Ópera

Local Reads

The immensely popular Arturo Perez-Reverte has written a few books set in Madrid, which make great accompaniments to a visit. Try the trilogy based on the adventures of the sword-fighting 17th-century Capitán Alatriste, whose footsteps you can follow in a walking tour (p38), or the suspense-filled *The Flanders Panel*, an art-world and historical thriller. Other worthy reads with a local and artistic flavour include Robert Hughes' excellent biography *Goya* and Gijs van Hensbergen's *Guernica: Biography of a Twentieth-Century Icon*.

Books, books and more books are on the menu at Panta Rhei

GUY MOBERLY

DEPARTMENT & CONVENIENCE STORES

ABC Serrano (4, F4)
Housed in a beautiful Mudéjar-style building in fashionable Salamanca, this excellent mall has five levels of shops (men's and women's fashion, homewares, gifts) and a space for eating.
☎ 91 577 50 31 ✉ Calle de Serrano 61 ⏱ 10am-

RICHARD NEBESKY

9pm Mon-Sat Ⓜ Rubén Dario, Serrano

El Corte Inglés (3, D3)
Behold the mother lode! A national institution and the embodiment of the one-stop shop, El Corte Inglés deserves a round of applause for seeming to stock everything you could possibly think of. Clothes, underwear, footwear, books, music, tickets for various events, electrical appliances and furnishings are all represented, and there are well over a dozen handy branches throughout town.
☎ 91 418 88 00 ✉ Calle Preciados 3 ⏱ 10am-10pm Mon-Sat Ⓜ Sol

El Jardín de Serrano (4, F6) As shopping malls go, this one's in the small but perfectly formed

category. It's high-end stuff, and mostly covers the fashion side, with a smattering of accessories. Pop into the inhouse Mallorca café to refuel on tea and cakes, all while gazing at the garden.
☎ 91 577 00 12 ✉ Calle de Goya 6 ⏱ 10am-10pm Mon-Sat Ⓜ Serrano

VIPS (3, C2) You might shudder at the idea of coming to a shopping mecca like Madrid and having to visit a convenience store, but hey, we've all got to do it at some point. VIPS branches are scattered throughout the city, with a range of items (magazines, condoms, tampons, maps) plus a café and film development.
☎ 91 559 66 21 ✉ Gran Vía 43 ⏱ 9am-3am Ⓜ Callao, Santo Domingo

DESIGN, HOMEWARES & GIFTS

Casa Yustas (3, D4) Gift shopping can be a real pain. Should you buy something practical, or buy something emblematic of where you've been? You can actually cover both bases here, with cute *castizo* (true-blue Madrileño) caps in all sizes and ceramic homewares. You can also find some laughably kitsch stuff if you want to provoke hilarity back home.
☎ 91 366 50 84 ✉ Plaza Mayor 30 ⏱ 9.30am-9.30pm Mon-Sat, 11am-9.30pm Sun Ⓜ Sol

El Transformista (2, B9) This very funky store stocks cool homewares and furnishings from the 1950s to the 1970s, with plenty of orange-hued knick-knacks making the hipster customers nostalgic for the décors they grew up with.
☎ 91 366 46 80 ✉ Calle de Mira el Rio Baja 18 ⏱ 10am-2pm & 5-8.30pm Mon-Sat, 10am-2pm Sun Ⓜ Puerta de Toledo

Habitat (4, F6) This is one of Spain's most popular home décor stores, with lots of furniture and furnishings

notable for bright colours, clean lines and decent prices.
☎ 91 181 26 00 ✉ Calle de la Hermosilla 18 ⏱ 10.30am-8.30pm Mon-Sat Ⓜ Serrano

Objetos de Arte Toledano (3, H5) An enormous emporium of Spanish arts, crafts and kitsch awaits shoppers just near the Prado. Yep, it's touristy, but the range is *huge*.
☎ 91 429 50 00 ✉ Paseo del Prado 10 ⏱ 9.30am-8pm Mon-Sat Ⓜ Banco de España

FASHION, CLOTHES & SHOES

Adolfo Dominguez (3, F2)
When we popped in, Adolfo Dominguez was doing a brisk trade with those wanting well-made, stylish clothes in natural fibres, with the odd twist thrown in. The shop itself is a beautiful old-fashioned temple of good taste at the stylish end of Gran Vía. ☎ 91 522 65 65 ✉ Gran Vía 11 🕓 10am-9pm Mon-Sat, noon-3pm & 4-8pm Sun Ⓜ Gran Vía

Camper (4, E6) Fight the hordes of Spaniards seeking comfort, and American college students seeking cool, to get to these shoes. With innovative designs, sturdy construction and all the colours of the rainbow represented in this shop, which closely resembles a trendy art gallery, a visit here ensures you're a happy Camper. ☎ 91 578 25 60 ✉ Calle de Serrano 24 🕓 10am-8.30pm Mon-Sat Ⓜ Colón, Serrano

Custo Barcelona (3, E2)
The now-iconic brightly patterned, boldly coloured T-shirts of Barcelona designer Custo Dalmau are artfully displayed in this chic modern shop. If the T-shirts don't grab you, maybe the funky bags and shoes (for men and women) will. ☎ 91 360 46 36 ✉ Calle de Fuencarral 29 🕓 10am-9pm Mon-Fri, 10am-10pm Sat Ⓜ Gran Vía

Deli Room (4, C6) With goods displayed like, you guessed it, a deli, we were hooked from the first moment. The stock consists of cutting-edge Spanish designers out to make a statement. Look out for the Ailanto and Miriam Ocariz labels in particular. ☎ 91 521 1983 ✉ Calle de Santa Bárbara 4 🕓 11am-2pm & 5-9pm Mon-Sat Ⓜ Tribunal

Ekseption (4, F6) Spain's most exclusive boutique has all the big names that 'fashionistas' love: Marni, Prada, Chloe, Dries Van Noten, Jean-Paul Gaultier and Dolce & Gabbana. You enter via a sleek Zen-style pebbled catwalk and depart with a serious case of fashionitis. ☎ 91 577 45 53 ✉ Calle de Velázquez 28

Fashions at H.A.N.D. (p44)

🕓 10.30am-2.30pm & 5-9pm Mon-Sat Ⓜ Velázquez

Excrupulous Net (3, H1)
The shoes here tend towards the very well made and the imaginative, with a great range from the excellent Muxart (Barcelona) brand for both men and women. English is spoken too. ☎ 91 521 72 44 ✉ Calle del Almirante 7 🕓 11am-2pm & 5.30-8.30pm Mon-Sat Ⓜ Chueca

Farrutx (2, D7) The antithesis of Camper shoes, Farrutx is where you come for flashy, killer heels that make you wonder if you'll be able to walk more than 5m once they're on. There's a range of bags on offer as well, a few party-pooping flats and some footwear for fellas. ☎ 91 577 09 24 ✉ Calle de Serrano 7 🕓 10am-2pm & 5.30-8.30pm Mon-Sat Ⓜ Retiro

Rebajas!
Anyone with an eye for a bargain will be salivating if they visit Madrid during sale time. Look for the word *rebajas* and get ready to exercise those credit cards. Everything is marked down from around mid-January to the end of February, and from the beginning of July until the end of August, with the discounts increasing as the sales draw to their conclusion (although the really good stuff gets snapped up very quickly!).

H.A.N.D (3, F2) The funky-with-a-twist clothes here lean towards the quirkier end of whatever's in fashion at this very minute and the two chaps at H.A.N.D are happy to help you put a look together. It's a nice-looking shop too, with some interesting colours and textures scattered about.
☎ 91 521 51 52
✉ Calle de Hortaleza 26
🕒 11am-9pm Mon-Sat
Ⓜ Gran Vía

Loewe (4, E6) If you're really into leather and like combining it with the high end of things, Loewe's your store. With a long-standing international reputation for buttery soft bags, wallets, belts and some seriously elegant fashions, you need never be out of leather if your heart so desires. Fabulous nonleather fashions are also available. There's a men's store nearby at No 34.
☎ 91 426 35 88
✉ Calle de Serrano 26
🕒 9.30am-8.30pm Mon-Sat Ⓜ Serrano

Mercado Fuencarral (3, F1) A one-stop collection of shops for those

Face to face with Zara

Going Dotty?
If you're in Madrid during any of the fiestas that see Madrileños don their finest traditional gear, you may develop a taste for ruffled polka-dot dresses, colourful shawls or black-and-white check caps. The area around Plaza Mayor is a good (if a little touristy) source of such gear, but our faves also include **Maty** (p48) and **Casa Jiménez** (p40). The less extravagant may simply want to tuck a carnation behind one ear.

itching to get their hands on streetwear and club-friendly fashions. Shoes, tops, bottoms, jewellery, sunglasses, bags and music can all be found, and a range of budgets is catered to. It certainly beats some of the tackier outlets on this particular strip.
☎ 91 521 41 52
✉ Calle de Fuencarral 45
🕒 11am-9pm Mon-Sat
Ⓜ Tribunal

Purificación Garcia (4, E6) The well-made clothes (sensibly fashionable and featuring interesting fabrics and colours) are allowed to shine in this modern layout. It's a good place for quality, special-occasion outfits and is very popular with local ladies.
☎ 91 576 72 76 ✉ Calle de Serrano 92 🕒 10am-8.30pm Mon-Sat
Ⓜ Serrano

Sportivo (4, A6) Label-lovin' casuals will want to move in here. Labels include Duffer of St George, Oeuf, Burro and Pringle. The range of shirts is particularly appealing, as is the friendly service.
☎ 91 542 56 61 ✉ Calle de Conde Duque 20

🕒 10am-2pm & 4-9pm Mon-Sat Ⓜ Noviciado

Underground (2, B9) With that authentic vintage-clothing store smell, Underground is a groovy place to scour the racks for preloved ballgowns, suede jackets, old-fashioned heels and funky tops. You'll find fashions from the 1950s to the very recent for men and women, plus some new stuff.
☎ 91 364 15 46 ✉ Calle Mira el Río Baja 14
🕒 10am-2.30pm & 5.30-8.30pm Mon-Fri, 10am-2.30pm Sat, 10.30am-3.30pm Sun
Ⓜ Puerta de Toledo

Zara (3, E2) This chain has branches all over Madrid. Zara's recipe for success involves churning out fashion-conscious knock offs of designer collections for men, women and children at very affordable prices. The store's popularity means items can get severely mauled, so before buying check things such as buttons, collars, zips and seams – and steer clear of Saturdays, which are bedlam.
☎ 91 521 12 83 ✉ Gran Vía 34 🕒 10am-8.30pm
Ⓜ Gran Vía

FOOD & DRINK

Bombonería Santa (4, F5)
A sweet tooth should be indulged at regular intervals, and this lovely shop will give you (and your dentist) plenty to work with. Selections can be packaged in gift boxes, which look almost as edible as their contents, and can hit the €100 mark with ease.
☎ 91 576 86 46 ✉ Calle de Serrano 56 ☯ 10am-2pm & 5-8pm Mon-Sat Ⓜ Serrano

Casa Mira (3, F4) *Turrón*, a nutty nougat treat that's queued for at Christmas time, can be tracked down here. Locals say it's the best, and we're inclined to agree, as the business has been in the same family's hands since 1842.
☎ 91 429 88 95 ✉ Carrera de San Jerónimo 30 ☯ 10am-2pm & 5-9pm Mon-Sat Ⓜ Sevilla

Lavinia (4, F5) This capacious, well-equipped store will set you right in your search for the perfect Spanish drop. You can also find wines from around the world. If you've remembered to pack your own bottle opener, you might like to wander to the park for an alfresco tipple.
☎ 91 426 06 04 ✉ Calle de José Ortega y Gasset 16 ☯ 10am-9pm Mon-Sat Ⓜ Núñez de Balboa

Licorilandia (3, F5) No need to carry a large bottle in your handbag; since 1964 this retro-looking shop has dedicated itself to providing all the miniature bottles of sherry, brandy, whisky and liquor anyone could ever want. Find Torres brandy, Tío Pépe *fino* (fine) and Cuban rum in dainty, tipple-sized serves.
☎ 91 429 12 57 ✉ Calle de León 30 ☯ 9.30am-2pm & 5-8.30pm Mon-Sat Ⓜ Antón Martín

Mallorca (2, D7) A fantastic spot to pick up delicious goodies as gifts or as snacks on the run, Mallorca has a great range of cheeses, meats, pastries, alcohol and some mouthwatering tapas. You pay for your goods at the cash register, handing over a small plastic board where scoffed purchases have been recorded. Ingenious! There are other branches throughout Madrid.
☎ 91 577 18 59 ✉ Calle de Serrano 6 ☯ 9.30am-9pm Ⓜ Retiro

Museo del Jamón (3, E4)
Only the Spanish can call a ham shop a *'museo'*, but then again, it looks like every single pig in Spain has donated a leg. There are branches throughout the city, and it's a good place to assuage hunger pains (vegetarians look elsewhere) or ponder how to get a big fat pig leg past customs.
☎ 91 521 03 46 ✉ Carrera de San Jerónimo 6 ☯ 9am-midnight Mon-Sat, 10am-midnight Sun Ⓜ Sol

Casa Mira is a house of miracles, with the city's best *turrón*

FOR CHILDREN

Caramelos Paco (3, C6)
Much as you tell them 'it'll rot your teeth', kids will be still be drawn to this treasure-trove of sweets, sweets and more sweets. And they are indeed delicious, although anyone who dreads putting kids to bed in the midst of a sugar rush might want to make sure that they purchase something from the sugar-free selection.
☎ 91 365 42 58
✉ Calle de Toledo 53
🕐 9.30am-2pm & 5-8.30pm Mon-Sat Ⓜ La Latina

Dideco (2, B9) Stock up on kids' toys (many of which may appeal to grown-ups) at Dideco, where you'll find everything: miniroller skates, inflatable pools, educational games, bath toys and art supplies. There are two other branches in Madrid.
☎ 91 365 02 40
✉ Mercado Puerta de Toledo, Ronda de Toledo 1
🕐 10.30am-9pm Tue-Sat, 10.30am-2.30pm Sun Ⓜ Puerta de Toledo

El Tintero Niños (3, G1)
Hunt out imaginative and colourful slogan T-shirts and romper suits for the baby or wee nipper in your life. Our past favourite? A red romper suit emblazoned with the phrase 'Enfant Terrible'. Grown-ups can shop at No 5.
☎ 91 310 44 02
✉ Calle de Gravina 9
🕐 10.30am-2pm & 5-9pm Ⓜ Chueca

Fiestas Paco (3, C6)
Jam-packed with all the prerequisites for a ripsnorter of a party, this is the place to come for lurid wigs, games and other sundries that will keep the littlies distracted for 10 minutes or so.
☎ 91 365 27 60 ✉ Calle de Toledo 52 🕐 9.30am-2pm & 5-8.30pm Mon-Fri, 9.30am-2pm Sat Ⓜ La Latina

Oilily (4, F6) Oilily is one of the swishest children's labels around, with great fabrics and colours plus very cool designs that will have more than a few adults wishing they could stretch the clothes a little. Not cheap, but duds will last until well and truly outgrown.
☎ 91 577 56 39 ✉ Calle de la Hermosilla 16
🕐 10am-8.30pm Mon-Sat Ⓜ Serrano

JEWELLERY, PERFUME & ACCESSORIES

Carrera y Carrera (4, E6)
Providing chunky diamonds and other precious-stone jawbreaker rings and jewels to the good ladies of Madrid since 1885, this store is known for service that is so silky smooth that staff will always be courteous and charming even if you're in the 'just looking' demographic.
☎ 91 577 05 72 ✉ Calle de Serrano 27 🕐 10am-2pm & 4.30-8.30pm Mon-Sat Ⓜ Serrano

Casa de Diego (3, E3)
A classic since 1858, this shop sells Spanish fans, shawls, umbrellas and canes. The grumpy old men who wait on you seem like they could have been around for the original shop's opening, but you might raise a smile if you send one of your own their way.
☎ 91 522 66 43
✉ Plaza de la Puerta del Sol 12 🕐 9.30am-2pm & 5-8pm Mon-Sat Ⓜ Sol

Piamonte (3, H1) This is the grown woman's equivalent to being a kid in a candy store, with mouth-watering bags available in all shapes and sizes and in any colour you care to mention. There's a great range of jewellery on offer too, as well as a judicious selection of truly funky threads. There are other branches throughout town.
☎ 91 308 48 62
✉ Calle de Marqués de Monasterio 5
🕐 10.30am-8.30pm Mon-Fri, 11am-8.30pm Sat Ⓜ Chueca

Casa de Diego has many fans

Sephora (3, E4) Feeling somewhat less than fragrant? Or looking for a mother lode of make-up? Sephora is a smartly black-and-white kitted-out store with all the big cosmetic ranges and what seems like 1000 smells. Look out for Perfumeria Gal lip glosses, a local brand

encased in some beautiful packaging.
☎ 91 523 71 71
✉ Plaza de Puerta del Sol 3 🕑 10am-9pm Mon-Sat Ⓜ Sol

women'secret (4, E6)
Hankering to be taken for a Madrileña? Then you'll have to start with the basics.

Spanish women love their scanties, and this groovy, up-to-the-minute store (part of a chain) has plenty, plus swimwear, kids' wear and seats for lingerie-weary chaps.
☎ 91 435 30 06
✉ Calle de Serrano 29
🕑 10am-8.30pm Mon-Sat Ⓜ Serrano

MARKETS

Cuesta de Moyano Bookstalls (3, J6) Every now and again, you may find an undiscovered gem at this market, full of second-hand and new books in many languages. As featured in Arturo Perez-Reverte's *The Nautical Chart*.
✉ Calle Claudio Moyano 🕑 9am-dusk Mon-Sat, 9am-2pm Sun Ⓜ Atocha

Mercadillo Marqués de Viana (2, C2) Nicknamed El Rastrillo (the Little Rastro) this is a calmer version of the big one. It's good fun all

the same and attracts lots of locals.
✉ Calle del Marqués de Viana 🕑 9am-2pm Sun Ⓜ Tetuán

Mercadillo Plaza de las Comendadores (4, A5) Madrid's markets usually take place in the morning to early afternoon, but this one allows the night owl to get among it and sort through some trash and treasure. There are plenty of handicrafts of varying quality.
✉ Plaza de las Comendadores

🕑 6-10pm Sat Ⓜ Noviciado

Mercado de San Miguel (3, C4) If you're self-catering, then this is the market for you. Though quite small, it's not a bad spot to seek out fresh fruit and vegetables and is also a good place to pick up a quick lunch or just have a look at some rather attractive produce. The building itself is a well-restored wrought-iron structure.
✉ Plaza de San Miguel 🕑 9am-2pm & 5-8pm Mon-Sat Ⓜ Sol

MUSIC

Bangladesh (3, C3)
Calle de la Costanilla de los Ángeles is lined with CD and music shops. For a wide selection of vinyl, including singles, hard-to-find records and collector's items, head to Bangladesh. If you don't see what you're looking for, just ask the friendly staff.
☎ 91 559 50 56
🖥 www.bangladesh discos.com in Spanish
✉ Calle de la Costanilla de los Ángeles 5
🕑 10.30am-2.30pm

& 5-8.30pm Mon-Sat Ⓜ Ópera, Santo Domingo

El Flamenco Vive (3, B4)
Flamenco aficionados and novices alike take note: this store is devoted to the subject of flamenco dance and music. There are books, CDs, instruments and costumes. The knowledgeable staff can point you in the direction of Madrid's best flamenco *tablao* (places) as well.
☎ 91 547 39 17 🖥 www .elflamencovive.com in Spanish ✉ Calle

de Conde de Lemos 7
🕑 10.30am-2pm & 5-9pm Mon-Sat Ⓜ Ópera

El Real Musical (3, B3)
Its location near the Teatro Real should be a give away as to what kind of musical tastes are catered for here. Yep, it's classical all the way, with sheet music, CDs, books and instruments temptingly arranged.
☎ 91 541 30 07 ✉ Calle de Carlos III 1 🕑 10am-2.15pm & 4.30-8pm Mon-Sat Ⓜ Ópera

SPECIALIST STORES

Amantis (4, D6) With a wide variety of lubricants, condoms, underwear, games, books and penisy things, Amantis is a popular sex shop with the gay crowd of Chueca and couples looking to liven things up.
☎ 91 702 05 10
✉ Calle de Pelayo 46
🕑 10.30am-10pm Mon-Sat, 4-9pm Sun
Ⓜ Chueca

Capas Seseña (3, E4) Madrid's winter will get you in the mood to rug up, and this shop will make nothing less than the best seem a necessity. The capes here are beautifully made and, despite the 1766 attempts by Esquillace (an unpopular minister during the reign of Carlos III) to make capes (at least long ones) illegal in Madrid, you'll attract nothing but envious glances if you don one, à la Hilary Clinton. Expect to pay around €400 for a deluxe model.
☎ 91 531 68 40 ✉ Calle de la Cruz 23 🕑 10am-2pm & 4.30-8pm Mon-Fri, 10am-2pm Sat Ⓜ Sol

Corsetería La Latina (3, C6) The largest bras, girdles and knickers you'll ever see (honest, look in the window at the mind-boggling display) steal the show on Calle de Toledo. If you've got problem boobs, this is definitely the place to find a home for them.
☎ 91 365 46 22 ✉ Calle de Toledo 49 🕑 10am-1.30pm & 5-8pm Mon-Fri, 10am-1.30pm Sat Ⓜ La Latina

Marihuana (3, D6) Forgotten to pack your bong? Then Marihuana may be of help. Packed to the gills with smokers' requisites (mostly of the dope-smoking variety) and rock T-shirts, it attracts young crowds when El Rastro's on, and while not as edgy as in the past (Sting was on the stereo when we last visited!), it's still a trip down short-term memory lane for some.
☎ 91 467 35 92 ✉ Plaza de Cascorro 6 🕑 10am-2pm & 5-8.30pm Mon-Sat, 10am-2pm Sun Ⓜ La Latina

Maty (3, D3) Everything you could ever need for flamenco performance can be found here, from heels and ruffled dresses to videos and DVDs for inspiration, as well as information on classes. It's not a bad spot for fellas to pick up some check caps either.
☎ 91 531 32 91 ✉ Calle de Maestro Victoria 2 🕑 10am-1.45pm & 5-8.30pm Mon-Fri, 10am-2pm & 5-8pm Sat Ⓜ Sol

Sobrinos de Perez (3, D4) This shop can supply you with everything your sacred heart may desire, from rosary beads to garishly-coloured statues of all the big-name saints. Everything's got a Catholic edge, but if you're looking for nothing more than kitsch, don't make it too obvious.
☎ 91 521 19 54 ✉ Calle de Postas 6 🕑 10am-2pm & 4.30-8pm Mon-Sat Ⓜ Sol

Give thanks for the heavenly items at Sobrinos de Perez

GUY MOBERLY

Eating

It's only fitting that Madrid, at the centre of Spain, should offer a distillation of Spanish cuisine of all types. This is thanks to its status as a city of Spanish immigrants bringing with them Asturian, Andalucian, Basque, Navarran, Catalan, Valencian, Murcian and Galician (among others) cooking styles. It also offers some great international cuisines, with Mediterranean, Asian, Middle Eastern, Mexican and North African widely available. Perhaps most surprisingly, Madrid is a great spot for seafood, with ocean catches transported daily to the capital for the hungry hordes!

Grazers will love the ritual of the tapas crawl and sampling titbits in such a social way. Big eaters will love the long, hearty lunches washed down with wine and punctuated by animated conversation.

Meal Costs

The pricing symbols used in this chapter indicate the cost of a three-course meal with a drink. For tapas joints, it's two portions and a drink.

$	under €15
$$	€16–25
$$$	€26–40
$$$$	over €41

Menú del Día

Every restaurant in Madrid will have (by law) its version of the *menú del día* – a set-lunch menu offering three courses and a drink. They cost about half as much as three courses and a drink from the à la carte menu, and are a great way to refuel Madrid-style (over about three hours!) for a reasonable price.

Dining Hours & Booking

Madrileños love to eat and they love to eat late! Most of them will have three or four courses for lunch (never before 2pm, and it will generally last until 4pm), and no-one will even consider dinner before 10pm. Get into the rhythm of the city's dining habits and you'll have a lot more fun.

A lot of places close on Sunday (and public holidays) and quite a few places close for part of August – or all of it. Still, there's no reason to think you'll starve. Because dining out is so popular here, you'd be well advised to make reservations for more expensive restaurants, especially at weekends or for lunch. Credit cards are widely accepted, although inexpensive restaurants generally accept cash only.

LOS AUSTRIAS & CENTRO

Casa Ciriaco (3, B4) $$$
Castillian
Frequented by families, business folk, and amateur artists (look at the walls), the food here is unpretentious and filling. Cluey waiters wear white jackets and will even give your shirt a squirt of stain remover if you've been sloppy with the *sopa* (soup).
☎ 91 548 06 20 ✉ Calle Mayor 84 ✇ 1.30-4.30pm & 8.30-11.30pm Thu-Tue Ⓜ Ópera

Casa Labra (3, D3) $
Tapas
Since 1860, Madrileños have been squeezing past each other in Casa Labra to get a beer in one hand and some *bacalao croquetas* in the other. Perhaps they were just the sort of inspiration needed for Pablo Iglesias and his comrades to found the Spanish socialist party here over 120 years ago. There's a restaurant ($$$) out the back too.
☎ 91 532 14 05 ✉ Calle de Tetuán 11 ✇ 9.30am-3.30pm & 6-11pm Mon-Sat Ⓜ Sol

Casa Paco (3, C5) $$$
Madrileña
This charming old-style place specialises in *madrileña* cooking, and the meat and egg dishes come highly recommended (especialy the steak). You're firmly in *castizo* territory here, so throw out the dietary restrictions and get busy loosening your belt. Oh, and make a reservation.
☎ 91 366 31 66 ✉ Plaza de Puerta Cerrada 11 ✇ 1.30-4pm & 8.30pm-midnight Mon-Sat Ⓜ Sol

Restaurante Sobrino de Botín (3, C4) $$$$
Castillian
We wonder if people even notice the food here, so busy are they soaking up all the history. Restaurante Sobrino is dubbed the oldest restaurant in the world. It's also featured in some well-known novels: Pérez Galdós' *Fortunata y Jacinta* and Hemingway's *The Sun Also Rises*. Yep, you could say it's a bit of a tourist trap, but it's an essential trap all the same, with suckling pig and excellent roast lamb.
☎ 91 366 42 17 ✉ Calle de los Cuchilleros 17 ✇ 1-4pm & 8pm-midnight Ⓜ Sol, Tirso de Molina ♿

Madrid's Cuisine

Tapas will provide you with some of your fondest memories of Madrid. Tapas are a way of eating, and therefore a way of socialising and forging (or reinforcing) relationships.

The word itself means lid, or top. The verb *tapar* means to top or to cover, and most people believe that the origin of tapas was in the 18th century, when tavern keepers would place a slice of ham or bread on the mouth of a glass to keep the flies out. It's also the best way of soaking up alcohol on a night out!

You'll find tapas in almost every bar in Madrid (larger portions are known as *raciones*). A few of the most common nibbling options:

Albóndigas meatballs

Bacalao cod

Boquerones fresh anchovies marinated in wine vinegar

Callos tripe

Chorizo spicy red cooked sausage

Gambas al ajillo prawns cooked in garlic-laden olive oil

Jamón ham

Morcilla blood sausage (fried)

Pulpo gallego spicy boiled octopus

Tortilla española potato & onion omelette

Taberna La Bola (3, B2) $$$

Madrileña

This tavern is well-known locally for its traditional *cocido a la madrileña* (a stew of vegetables, chickpeas, chicken, beef, lard and perhaps sausage) and has been placating hungry Madrileño tummies since 1880. There's a very nice old-fashioned atmosphere here, with good old-fashioned service, and the high turnover is always an excellent sign.

☎ 91 547 69 30 ✉ Calle de la Bola 5 ⌚ 1.30-4pm & 8.30pm-midnight Mon-Sat, 1.30-4pm Sun Ⓜ Santo Domingo ♿

Enjoy a pig out at Restaurante Sobrino de Botín

GUY MOBERLY

SOL, HUERTAS & SANTA ANA

Arrocería Galá (3, G5) $$$

Paella/Valencian

Make a reservation for this place as soon as you arrive in Madrid. Even so, you might not get a table until about 4pm for lunch, but the rich rice dishes, glass-covered atrium, friendly service and general conviviality of everyone around you make it worth the wait. Credit cards not accepted.

☎ 91 429 25 62 ✉ Calle de Moratín 22 ⌚ 2-5pm & 9pm-1.30am Ⓜ Antón Martín ♿

Casa Alberto (3, F5) $

Tapas

With pics, paintings and tiles on the walls plus fancy woodwork, this is a great spot to nibble tapas while slaking a beer or *vermut* (vermouth) thirst. Service is courteous and you can eat in the restaurant ($$$) at

the back if you hanker for something more substantial, such as bull's-tail stew.

☎ 91 429 93 56 ✉ Calle de las Huertas 18 ⌚ noon-5.30pm & 8pm-1.30am Tue-Sat, noon-5.30pm Sun Ⓜ Antón Martín

East 47 (3, G4) $$$$

Creative

Both a restaurant and a stylish bar, this reflects its parent, the Hotel Villa Real (p70), as it has a feeling of luxury without being predictable. The meat dishes are strong, there's plenty to tempt caviar lovers and the wine list is worth exploring.

☎ 91 420 37 67 ✉ Hotel Villa Real, Plaza de las Cortes 10 ⌚ 11am-1am Ⓜ Banco de España

El Caldero (3, F5) $$$

Murcian

All muted earth-tones and cuisine from Murcia, this

place does a wicked line of rice-based dishes for two. The *dorada a la sal* (rock-salt crusted dory) or *arroz negro* (rice with squid ink) are excellent choices, but attentive staff will help the indecisive.

☎ 91 429 50 44 ✉ Calle de las Huertas 15 ⌚ 1.30-4pm & 9pm-midnight Tue-Sat, 1.30-4pm Mon & Sun Ⓜ Antón Martín

El Cenador del Prado (3, F4) $$$

Creative

When your eyes get used to the riot of red, purple and pink near the entrance, you'll probably get taken to a cool, light-filled atrium, where exceptionally prescient service awaits, along with a wonderful modern menu (and a choice of degustation menus – including vegetarian) and lavish desserts.

Expect a crowd of politicos from down the road.

☎ 91 429 15 61 ✉ Calle del Prado 4 ☾ 1.30-4pm & 9pm-midnight Mon-Sat, 1-4pm Sun Ⓜ Antón Martín, Sol Ⓥ

La Bio Tika (3, G5) $
Vegetarian
Feeling that your food pyramid's been turned upside-down? Try this place – the healthy (and flavoursome) cuisine is vegetarian and macrobiotic, service is calm and casual, and the no-smoking policy is a bonus. Cash only.

☎ 91 429 07 80 ✉ Calle Amor de Dios 3 ☾ 1-4.30pm & 8-11.30pm Mon-Fri, 1.30-4.30pm Sat & Sun Ⓜ Antón Martín ♿ Ⓥ ✖

La Finca de Susana (3, F4) $
Mediterranean
Incredible value, given the modern, attractive décor and imaginative dishes, but it's no secret. Get in early, or join a long queue. The *menú del día* is extraordinary for €7.75, but off-the-menu ordering (such as the *tajines de verdura con gambas a la vinagreta de mostaza* – *tagine* with vegetables, prawns and a mustard vinaigrette) will deliver the same happy surprise.

☎ 91 369 35 57 ✉ Calle de Arlabán 4 ☾ 1-3.45pm & 8.30-11.45pm Ⓜ Sevilla Ⓥ

La Trucha (3, F4) $
Tapas
This is one of Madrid's best spots for tapas, especially if it's Andalucian under stark

fluoro lighting that you're after. The seafood nibbles are truly scrumptious, but you can also eat out the back if you're after something more substantial. There's another branch at Calle de Núñez de Arce 6 (3, E4).

☎ 91 429 58 33 ✉ Calle de Manuel Fernández y González 3 ☾ 1-4pm & 8pm-midnight Ⓜ Sol, Sevilla

La Vaca Verónica (3, H5) $$$
Mediterranean
The ladies of La Vaca Verónica understand that good eating lies in the freshest, finest ingredients, simply prepared Argentinian-style – sardines are plump and juicy, and the steaks are wonderfully cooked to a perfect medium rare. The décor is yellow-hued, with a few chandeliers thrown in, although this little touch doesn't make it feel stuffy. Reservations are advised at the weekend.

☎ 91 429 78 27 ✉ Calle Moratín 38 ☾ noon-4pm & 9pm-midnight Sun-Fri, 9pm-midnight Sat Ⓜ Antón Martín

Las Bravas (3, E4) $
Tapas
Las Bravas specialises in *patatas bravas* (crispy potato with a tomato-chilli sauce) – so much so, that its sauce is patented (No 357492 if you're wondering). The décor is nothing to write home about, but the spuds are an attraction for locals and tourists alike.

☎ 91 532 26 20 ✉ Callejón de Álvarez Gato 3 ☾ 10am-11.30pm Ⓜ Sol ♿ Ⓥ

Lhardy (3, E4) $$$$
Tapas/French/Madrileña
A staple of swanky Madrid since 1839, this is the place for high-end tapas, French cuisine – try the *perdiz estofado* (partridge stew) – and some excellent local dishes, including *callos* (tripe). Impressive setting too, with the upper walls displaying what was once the royal family's banqueting service.

☎ 91 522 22 07 ✉ Carrera de San Jerónimo 8 ☾ 1-3.30pm & 8.30-11.30pm Mon-Sat, 1-3.30pm Sun Ⓜ Sol, Sevilla

Los Gatos (3, G5) $
Tapas
Like a mission-brown explosion in a bullfighting-kitsch factory, this place brings new meaning to the phrase 'cheek by jowl'. If you're lucky, you'll see the overworked grill on fire when tapas overload occurs. A definite fave, especially the *anguilas* (little eels on toast).

☎ 91 429 30 67 ✉ Calle de Jesús 2 ☾ noon-1am Mon-Thu & Sun, noon-2am Fri & Sat Ⓜ Antón Martín

Olsen (3, F4) $$$
Scandinavian
The lunchtime *menú del día* boasts more Mediterranean flavours than you might expect, but delve a little deeper and you'll come up with a fist full of salmon in one hand and one hell of a vodka list in the other. The décor is all blonde wood, attractive lighting and nice cutlery, as you'd expect.

☎ 91 429 36 59 ✉ Calle del Prado 15 ☾ 1-4pm & 8.30pm-midnight Tue-Sun Ⓜ Sevilla

LA LATINA & LAVAPIÉS

Asador Frontón
(3, D5) $$$
Basque
Nostrils and tastebuds start twitching with thoughts of this place (head upstairs from Calle de Jesús y María once you spy the canary-yellow building on grotty Plaza Tirso de Molina) and its charcoal-grilled meat and fish dishes. While the desserts may be too heavy after carnivorous festivities (the T-bone steak needs its own postcode), the wine selection ensures you're getting more than just one food group – well, sorta.
☎ 91 369 16 17 ⊠ Plaza Tirso de Molina 7 ⏲ 1.30-4pm & 9pm-midnight Mon-Sat, 1.30-4pm Sun Ⓜ Tirso de Molina

Casa de Tostas (2, C9) $$
Tapas
Lavapiés residents know there's no point in socialising without getting stuck into *tostas* (toasts), and the ones here (€5.75 each) are pretty hefty (although the prices have skyrocketed over the last few years). Generous serves, with a great range of toppings (the *pate de bacalao* is our favourite),

and the place is full of a lot of happy munchers.
☎ 91 527 08 42
⊠ Calle de Argumosa 29
⏲ 1-4pm & 6pm-1am
Ⓜ Lavapiés ⚬

Casa Lucio (3, B6) $$$$
Madrileña
Casa Lucio remains a firm favourite for those who like to partake of well-prepared *madrileña* dishes, such as *revuelto* (scrambled eggs), *callos* (tripe) and *arroz con leche* (rice pudding) – that is, comfort food, local-style. The place is casual and welcoming, but can get busy, so you might have to stand at the bar for a while and wait for a table to be vacated.
☎ 91 365 32 52 ⊠ Calle de la Cava Baja 35

Vegetarian Options
Madrid loves its meat, but there are plenty of places to tuck into vegetarian food. The Ⓥ indicates that a place is either fully vegetarian or has an excellent selection of vegetarian dishes. The following offer specifically vegetarian dining:
Chez Pomme (p55)
El Estragón (below)
Isla del Tesoro (p55)
La Bio Tika (opposite)

⏲ 1-4pm & 9-11.30pm Sun-Fri, 9-11.30pm Sat
Ⓜ La Latina ⚬

El Almendro 13 (3, B5) $$
Tapas
Don't get people started on the topic of the *huevos rotos* (broken eggs – a bit like scrambled eggs) here – they'll never stop. Just get started on the eggs themselves! Excellent tapas, a great rustic atmosphere, and very good wines make this place extremely popular, particularly on weekends.
☎ 91 365 42 52 ⊠ Calle del Almendro 13 ⏲ 1-4pm & 7pm-midnight
Ⓜ La Latina ⚬

El Estragón (3, B5) $$
Vegetarian
With the delightful Plaza de la Paja as a good spot to start off a social whirl, the standard vegetarian food (the crepes are popular) of this long-time fave should see you sated. Staff are kind, and there's a non-smoking room too.
☎ 91 365 89 82
⊠ Plaza de la Paja 10
⏲ 1.30-5pm & 8.30pm-midnight Ⓜ La Latina
Ⓥ ✄

Dine on both food groups (meat and wine) at Asador Frontón

GUY MOBERLY

Juana la Loca (3, B6) $$
Tapas

The only thing crazy here is how crowded it can get with La Latina revellers looking for inspired, sublime *pintxos* (Basque tapas). Any of the canapés are moreish, but *raciones* such as the *carpaccio* (thin slices of raw beef) will see a fork battle waged at your table with fellow diners. ☎ 91 364 05 25 ✉ Plaza Puerto de Moros 4 🕒 noon-5pm & 8pm-2am Ⓜ La Latina

Julián de Tolosa (3, C5) $$$$
Navarran

A charmingly rustic-meets-modern atmosphere pervades this Navarran institution. Think lots of exposed brick and timber and solid batten-the-hatches food, perfectly executed. Beans are a green feature on the menu, and if you want something to break up all

that fibre, have a *chuletón* (enormous chop). Reservations are essential, especially on weekends and at lunch. ☎ 91 365 82 10 ✉ Calle de la Cava Baja 18 🕒 1-4.30pm & 8.30pm-midnight Mon-Sat, 1-4.30pm Sun Ⓜ La Latina

Posada de la Villa (3, C5) $$$$
Madrileña

A wonderfully restored 17th-century inn where all sorts of people, from travel-ling salesmen to fellows of ill repute, were purported to have sought lodging. History lesson dispatched, tuck into the classic *madrileña* fare, such as the suckling pig and a distinct lack of vegetarian options. Don't even think about Sunday lunch here without making a reservation. ☎ 91 366 18 60 ✉ Calle de la Cava Baja 9 🕒 1-4pm & 8pm-midnight Mon-Sat, 1-4pm Sun Ⓜ La Latina

All sorts love Posada de la Villa's, except vegetarians and pigs

MALASAÑA & CHUECA

Azul Profundo (3, G1) $$$
Tapas/Creative

This 'deep blue' joint shares a colour scheme with next-door's discount shop and has adopted an inventive approach to the serious business of eating. The main option is a set menu of varied and creative tapas (€35) by one of the hottest young chefs in town, Andrés Madrigal. The portions are so pretty it seems a shame to sully them with a knife. ☎ 91 532 25 64 ✉ Calle de Plaza de Chueca 4 🕒 1-4pm & 8pm-midnight Tue-Sat, 1-4pm Sun Ⓜ Chueca

Bar Casa do Compañeiro (4, B6) $
Tapas

The fried *morcilla* (black pudding) here is served with a few hunks of bread. It's not fine dining but it is extremely tasty and certainly does the trick as a stomach liner before a boozy night in the barrio. And the good Galician smiles we got warmed our hearts. ☎ 91 521 57 02 ✉ Calle de San Vicente Ferrer 44 🕒 1pm-2am Ⓜ Noviciado, Tribunal

Bazaar (3, G2) $$
Mediterranean/Creative

A blindingly white shabby-chic space on a sought-after corner location means this is Chueca dining at its most chichi. Expect a nattily dressed youngish crowd and creative, well-prepared dishes that make the most of the Mediterranean's ingredients and sunny climate. Very cool, despite having Rod Stewart on the stereo when we visited. Reservations not accepted. ☎ 91 523 39 05 ✉ Calle de la Libertad 21 🕒 noon-4pm & 8pm-midnight Ⓜ Chueca

Café Comercial (4, C5) $
Café

A local institution of the best kind! The Café Comercial has been a meeting place, a *tertulia* (chat session) centre and breakfast spot for donkeys' years. Grab a coffee and a pastry or a snack, and people-watch from behind a newspaper. If the food's not enough, come for the litter-strewn décor.
☎ 91 521 56 55 ✉ **Glorieta de Bilbao 7** ◷ **8am-1am Sun-Thu, 8am-2am Fri & Sat** Ⓜ **Bilbao**

Chez Pomme (3, G1) $$
Vegetarian

A smart-looking place, with a loyal clientele from the gay community, Chez Pomme serves up tasty vegetarian morsels and substantial mains, all without ramming earth-tones down your throat, as so many healthy places do. The *menú del día* is excellent value.
☎ 91 532 16 46 ✉ **Calle de Pelayo 4** ◷ **1.30-4.30pm & 8.30-11.30pm Mon-Sat** Ⓜ **Chueca** Ⓥ ✂

El Pepinillo de Barquillo (4, D6) $$$
Creative Spanish

Humorous touches (such as the giant gherkin hanging from the ceiling) don't detract from the seriously good food, which combines fresh ingredients with old faves such as *solomillo* (steak) and *ventresca* (tuna). Apparently, this place is good for star-spotting but we think it's the redoubtable Ángela, the chef, who's the star.
☎ 91 310 25 46 ✉ **Calle del Barquillo 42** ◷ **1-5pm & 8.30pm-2am** Ⓜ **Chueca** Ⓥ

Gran Café de Gijón (3, H1) $$$
Café/International

This long-time haunt of literary Madrid has been dishing up coffee, good meals and blood-red velvet décor since 1888. In the winter months, the atmosphere is cosy – in summer you should head outside to the swanky terrace area, where a grand piano sits ready to serenade you, and *cava* (champagne) lightly bubbles away ready to quench your thirst.
☎ 91 521 54 25 ✉ **Paseo de los Recoletos 21** ◷ **7am-2am** Ⓜ **Banco de España, Chueca**

Isla del Tesoro (4, C5) $$
Vegetarian

This delightful little joint serves very good vegetarian food with a great deal of flair, fun and frivolity. The staff are cheery and the crowds are far from pious, plus the 'treasure island' feel of the décor will make you smile. We also dig the big purple-velvet double bass that you'll see just hanging around.
☎ 91 593 14 40 ✉ **Calle de Manuela Malasaña 3** ◷ **1-4pm & 9-11.30pm** Ⓜ **Bilbao** Ⓥ

La Dame Noire (3, F2) $$$
French

This lavish, theatrically decorated restaurant (think blood-red curtains, lots of gilt and flattering candle-light) specialises in wonderfully rich French food (think *lengua de buey al vino de Madeira* – bull's tongue) and assiduously cultivated service, all to a typically French soundtrack of Piaf, Gainsbourg et al. Reservations are recommended.
☎ 91 531 04 76 ✉ **Calle de Perez Galdós 3** ◷ **9pm-1am Tue-Thu & Sun, 9pm-2.30am Fri & Sat** Ⓜ **Gran Vía**

La Musa (4, B5) $$
Market

A buzzing disco vibe fills this place even at lunch. Lunch also sees a handy *menú del día* that keeps the Malasaña locals full, satisfied and wanting to return. That and the fantastic fried green tomatoes topped

---

Sealing the Deal

If you're in Madrid for business, these are some good places to make an impression:
El Bodegon (p58)
El Cenador del Prado (p51)
Julián de Tolosa (opposite)
Paulino (p58)
Restaurante Oter Epicure (p57)
Santceloni (p58)
Zalacaín (p58)

with goats' cheese. It can seem overly crowded, but there's always a nearby plaza for recuperation and some fresh air.

☎ 91 448 75 58 ✉ Calle de Manuela Malasaña 18 🕑 9am-midnight Ⓜ Bilbao

La Panza es Primero (3, G1) $$
Mexican

Admire the Mexi-kitsch and get yourself settled with a Coronita (or perhaps a tequila) and a plump south-of-the-border taco or a tasty chicken dish. Service is friendly and fast, and the tacos are good for kids, as they can be ordered one at a time, with a range of fillings.

☎ 91 521 76 40 ✉ Calle de la Libertad 33 🕑 1pm-1am Ⓜ Chueca ♿

madrilia (3, F2) $$$
Mediterranean

The lower-case 'm' should give you a fairly good idea

of what you can expect from this place. Well-prepared straightforward pasta dishes are served up in slick, blue-lit surrounds to a smart yet hungry set. Not a bad spot for a light lunch.

☎ 91 523 92 75 ✉ Calle de Clavel 6 🕑 1-4pm & 8.30pm-midnight Ⓜ Gran Vía

Stop Madrid (3, F2) $$
Tapas

Stop Madrid from what? Gorging on delicious tapas? Not likely. This popular local spot gets busy in the afternoon and evening, and has some great wines. There are plenty of yellowing tiles, lots of dark wood and very warm service. Tapas is mostly *jamón*- and chorizo-based, and the tomato salad has plenty of fans.

☎ 91 523 54 42 ✉ Calle de Hortaleza 11 🕑 12.30-4pm & 6pm-2am Mon-Sat Ⓜ Gran Vía

GUY MOBERLY

Wokcafe (3, G2) $$
Asian

Chueca's always happy to embrace trends from elsewhere, and Wokcafe has proved popular for its quality Asian-influenced stir-fries. The décor avoids sterility thanks to the triffid-style greenery, spiralling lampshades and a beaten-gold wall.

☎ 91 522 90 69 ✉ Calle de las Infantas 44 🕑 10am-2am Mon-Sat Ⓜ Banco de España ♿ Ⓥ

SALAMANCA & RETIRO

Biotza (4, F6) $$
Basque

Hip, modern and self-assured, Biotza is a very worthy addition to the scene in Salamanca, with décor straight from the pages of an interior design mag, innovative Basque cuisine (*tempura de berenjeras* – aubergine tempura) available in the restaurant and excellent *pintxos* if you're only interested in a quick refuel for a shopping spree.

☎ 91 781 03 13 ✉ Calle de Claudio Coello 27

🕑 9am-midnight Mon-Thu, 9am-1am Fri & Sat Ⓜ Serrano

Café-Restaurante El Espejo (3, J1) $$$
Café/Basque/French

This café is an elegant spot to while away the hours. The *pabellón* (pavilion) is one of *the* places to have a tipple in summer, and it's all to a pianist's tinkling accompaniment. The more upmarket restaurant serves good Basque/French cuisine. Dress up and make a night of it.

☎ 91 308 23 47 ✉ Paseo de los Recoletos 31 🕑 8am-1am Ⓜ Colón

Mumbai Masala (3, J1) $$$
Indian

A contender for the title of Madrid's prettiest restaurant, the glittery décor at Mumbai Masala almost competes with the yummy northeast Indian cuisine. Dishes are packed with flavour (although not as spicy as you may be used to) and service is a joy. Book for weekends, as opening hours are relatively short, or wait in their bar next door.

☎ 91 435 71 94
✉ Calle de Recoletos 14
🕑 1.30-3.30pm
& 9-11pm Sun-Thu,
1.30-3.30pm & 9pm-
midnight Fri, 1.30-4pm
& 9pm-midnight
Sat Ⓜ Banco de
España Ⓥ

Restaurante Oter Epicure (4, F5) $$$$
Navarran

The food here is upmarket Navarran, with a bit of Basque thrown in too, just to ensure that everyone's satisfied. The service is smooth, the presentation reveals much effort, and the wine list is a thing of beauty. You might want to dress up and make a reservation.

☎ 91 431 67 71 ✉ Calle de Claudio Coello 73
🕑 1-4.30pm & 8.30pm-
midnight Mon-Sat
Ⓜ Serrano

Teatriz: dramatic décor, dining, and toilets

Caffeine Fix

Café con leche (drunk in the mornings only) is about half coffee, half hot milk. A *café solo* is a short black, while a *café cortado* is a short black with a dash of milk. For iced coffee, ask for a *café con hielo;* you'll be served a glass of ice and a hot cup of coffee to be poured over the ice.

Sushi Itto (3, J1) $$
Japanese

As neat and shiny as a new pin, but also casual enough to lose the 'Japanese shrine' atmosphere that can hamper the fun in many such restaurants, this place does great sushi and *gyoza* (dumplings), which can be shared or hogged according to your mood, or even delivered to your hotel.

☎ 91 426 21 69
✉ Calle de Recoletos 10
🕑 1.30-4.30pm &
8.30pm-midnight Sun-
Thu, 1.30-4.30pm
& 8.30pm-1am Fri &
Sat Ⓜ Banco de
España ♿

Taberna de la Daniela (2, E6) $$
Tapas

It's easy to overlook the Goya area if tapas and tipples are on your mind, but at midday, this well-tiled, colourful joint attracts quite a few people, and they all seem to be enjoying what's on offer, despite the fact that service is patchy at times.

☎ 91 575 23 29
✉ Calle del General Pardiñas 21 🕑 11.30am-
5.30pm & 7.30-
11.30pm Sun-Thu,
7.30pm-1am Fri & Sat
Ⓜ Goya

Teatriz (4, F6) $$$$
Creative

Even the toilets are a theatrical experience here – visitors leave luminous footprints on the floor. You'll be spending more than a penny though at this Philippe Starck–designed restaurant, as this has been one of Madrid's coolest for years. You'll certainly want to put on your glad rags, and reservations are definitely recommended.

☎ 91 577 53 79
✉ Calle de la Hermosilla 15 🕑 1.30-
4pm & 9pm-1am
Ⓜ Serrano ♿

Thai Gardens (4, F6) $$$$
Thai

The name says it all really. The good Thai food here shines in a lavish garden setting. Ingredients are fresh (they're flown in on a weekly basis from Thailand), graciously presented and skilfully handled, plus there's parking and the chance of spotting a Real Madrid star. You'd be well advised to make a reservation, especially at weekends.

☎ 91 577 88 84
✉ Calle de Jorge Juan 5 🕑 2-5pm daily,
9pm-1am Sun-Thu,
9pm-2am Fri & Sat
Ⓜ Serrano Ⓥ

RICHARD NEBESKY

ARGÜELLES & CHAMBERÍ

Casa Mingo (2, A7) $$
Asturian

Casa Mingo keeps things simple: chicken and cider, the Asturian way. It's a cheery, cheap and chipper place to enjoy a hearty lunch and a bit of history, as this place has been cidering up Madrileños since 1888.
☎ 91 547 79 18 ✉ Paseo de la Florida 34 🕒 11am–midnight Ⓜ Príncipe Pío

Paulino (4, B4) $$$$
Creative

Paulino occupies a cavernous exposed-brick-and-beams space, and is populated by efficient staff and hungry locals. The happy diners love tucking in to beautifully prepared dishes such as *solomillo a la parilla con raviolis de foie gras* (steak with foie gras ravioli) and washing it down with a little something from the sterling wine cellar. Excellent desserts too.
☎ 91 591 39 29 ✉ Calle de Jordán 7 🕒 noon–4pm & 8pm–midnight Mon–Sat Ⓜ Quevedo

Toma (4, A6) $$$
Creative

This is a modern, comfy and diminutive bistro (only six tables), where the chef's imagination is used to full effect but never brings out the emperor's new clothes. Not a bad spot to wander into for a cocktail either, although space is at a premium. Reservations are a damn good idea.
☎ 91 547 49 96 ✉ Calle de Conde Duque 14 🕒 9pm–1am Tue–Sat Ⓜ Plaza de España

NORTHERN MADRID

Combarro (2, C3) $$$$
Galician

Combarro offers its diners first-quality Galician seafood, especially *pulpo* (octopus). It's not the fanciest place, but it's very popular with business types and tourists who've asked the concierge at their five-star digs where they should go for seafood. You may have a bit of a wait, which is the perfect excuse to prop up the bar and imbibe, nibble and chat.
☎ 91 554 77 84 ✉ Calle de la Reina Mercedes 12 🕒 1.30–4pm & 8pm–midnight Mon–Sat, 1.30–4pm Sun Ⓜ Alvarado

El Bodegon (4, E3) $$$$
Basque/Catalan

El Bodegon has a strong reputation for excellent Basque cooking, a great wine list and old-fashioned service. Try the *rodaballo* (turbot) if it's on the menu – the traditional approach doesn't mean the chef's afraid to try new ingredients and techniques, and you shouldn't be either.
☎ 91 562 31 37 ✉ Calle del Pinar 15 🕒 1–4pm & 8pm–midnight Mon–Fri, 8pm–midnight Sat Ⓜ Gregorio Marañón

Santceloni (4, E3) $$$$
Creative Catalan

This smartly decorated yet comfortable Michelin-starred restaurant is in the basement of the Hesperia Hotel (p70). It's the sort of place that gourmands put ahead of anything else on their 'must do' list for Madrid. Superlatives just don't cut it; suffice to say that chef Santi Santamaría should be made the patron saint of exquisite food and the caviar with blinis (€65) could launch a thousand postcards. Reservations are essential, and easier to come by if you're a guest of the hotel.
☎ 91 210 88 40 ✉ Hesperia Castellana, Paseo de la Castellana 57 🕒 2–4pm & 9–11pm Mon–Fri, 9–11pm Sat Ⓜ Gregorio Marañón

Zalacaín (4, E3) $$$$
Creative

The proud possessor of three Michelin stars, Zalacaín is one of Madrid's finest restaurants. It was established by the Oyarbide family in the 1970s, and standards have not slipped, so dress up (coat and tie for chaps), unhinge the wallet and get busy with the menu (after having reserved a table well in advance).
☎ 91 561 59 35 ✉ Calle Álvarez de Baena 4 🕒 1.15–4pm & 9pm–midnight Mon–Fri, 9pm–midnight Sat Ⓜ Gregorio Marañón

Entertainment

The reason it's a cliché is because it's true – Madrileños really don't end the night until they've killed it. It's the perfect place for making merry, with a plethora of bars (more than 10,000), great gay nightlife, all-night-long dance clubs, and a whirl of flamenco, jazz, salsa and rock venues. If the more old-fashioned arts are your cup of tea, the theatre scene is lively, the opera is sterling, classical music is appreciated and modern dance, well, it's getting there. Locals love nothing more than going to the movies on a Sunday. All this plus local festivals and city-sponsored events means you can be busy indeed.

Locals are as passionate about social life as you've heard, and the hours they keep are startling. Don't even think about starting a big night before midnight. Dancing won't begin until around 3am. Bed time? About 6am – well, maybe.

Tickets & Listings

The weekly *Guía del Ocio* (€1) is a must for keeping abreast of what's on. The free English-language rag, *In Madrid,* is also a good source of information, while tourist offices can help with tracking down events and will have information on the arts scene. You can also try *El País* and *El Mundo,* which publish entertainment listings.

Tickets for plays, concerts and other performances can be bought at the theatre concerned, and a few lottery-ticket booths sell theatre, football and bullfight tickets. **FNAC** (3, D2; ☎ 91 595 62 00; www.fnac

> **Top Spots**
> Madrid's top nightlife area surrounds the Plaza de Santa Ana, with literally hundreds of bars and thousands of people, from the young to the not-so-young and from the avowedly local to a variety of nationalities. Other popular areas include Malasaña, which attracts a grungy, youthful crowd; Chamberí for lots of teens; and La Latina, with a good mix of traditional and quirky nightspots. The upwardly mobile set generally frequents the Salamanca barrio, while lovers of gay nightlife flock to Chueca.

RICHARD NEBESKY

.es in Spanish) sells tickets to major concerts and other events. **El Corte Inglés** (3, D3; ☎ 91 379 80 00; www.elcorteingles.es in Spanish) has tickets to almost all events in the city. You can also get tickets in **Servicaixa's ATMs** (☎ 90 233 22 11; www.servicaixa.com in Spanish).

Telephone and Internet bookings are also possible. Try the **Caixa de Catalunya** (☎ 90 210 12 12; www.telentrada.com), with tickets to many major events and concerts, and **Entradas.com** (☎ 90 248 84 88; www.entradas.com in Spanish), which also sells cinema tickets. Like all credit-card bookings, you pay by card and then collect the tickets from the relevant venue.

Special Events

January *New Year's Eve* – People eat a grape for each chime of the clock in Plaza de la Puerta del Sol, for good luck.

Día de los Reyes Magos – On 6 January, a parade of the three kings winds its way around the city, to the delight of kids.

February–March *Carnevales* – Days of fancy-dress parades and merrymaking across the Comunidad de Madrid, usually ending on the Tuesday 47 days before Easter Sunday.

Flamenco Festival – Five days of fine flamenco music in one of the city's theatres (often the Teatro Albéniz, p66, but check). The dates are moveable.

Arco (www.arco.ifema.es) – One of Europe's biggest contemporary art fairs, this lasts for five days around the middle of February.

May *Fiesta de la Comunidad de Madrid* – Celebrations are kicked off on 2 May with a speech by a local personality from the balcony of the Casa de Correos in the Plaza de la Puerta del Sol, and a host of cultural events and festivities follow.

Fiestas de San Isidro – 15 May is the big one! The feast day of the city's patron saint is followed by a week of partying. The country's most prestigious *feria*, or bullfighting season, also begins now and continues for a month, at the Plaza de Toros Monumental de Las Ventas (p29).

June–July *Local Fiestas* – Most districts in Madrid celebrate the feast day of one saint or another; ask the tourist office for details of where and when these local knees-ups take place.

July–August *Veranos de la Villa* – Council-organised arts festival with something for everyone, day and night, whether it be film, dance, music, theatre, photography, art or fashion.

Fiestas de San Lorenzo, San Cayetano & La Virgen de la Paloma – These three local patron saints' festivities (which revolve around La Latina, Plaza de Lavapiés and Calle de Calatrava in La Latina, respectively) keep the central districts of Madrid busy for the best part of three weeks, from 27 July to 15 August.

Feast of the Assumption – 15 August is a solemn date in the city's religious calendar, celebrating the Assumption of the Virgin Mary.

September *Local Fiestas* – Local councils organise fiestas in the first and second weeks of September; these are very local affairs and provide a rare insight into barrio life of the average Madrileño.

Fiesta del PCE – In mid-September the Spanish Communist Party holds its annual fundraiser in the Casa de Campo, a weekend-long mixed bag of regional-food pavilions, rock concerts and political soap-boxing.

November *Día de la Virgen de la Almudena* – On 9 November *castizos* (true-blue Madrileños) gather in Plaza Mayor to hear Mass on this, the feast day of the city's female patron saint.

December *Navidad (Christmas)* – Family time. Many celebrate with a big midday meal, although some prefer to eat on Christmas Eve *(Nochebuena)*. Nativity scenes (cribs) are set up in churches around the city and an exhibition of them is held in Plaza Mayor.

BARS

Antik Café (3, F2) This is a lovely little bar with ostentatious décor flourishes such as leopard print and lots of gilt, and a cheery crowd of Chueca types and lounge lizards. A mean hot chocolate with a shot of brandy is the perfect antidote to a cold day, while a mean cocktail makes a hot night even hotter.
☎ 620 427 168 ⊠ Calle de Hortaleza 4 & 6 ⓥ 10am-3am Ⓜ Gran Vía

Bar Cock (3, F2) Once a salon for high-class prostitution, Bar Cock retains a gentlemen's club atmosphere, though the crowd is often comprised of resolutely with-it 30-somethings in linen, leather, lace and polo-neck sweaters. You have to knock to get in, and look the part. Drinks are stiff, as you'd expect from a place with such a name.
☎ 91 532 28 26 ⊠ Calle de la Reina 16 ⓥ 7pm-3am Mon-Thu, to 3.30am Fri & Sat Ⓜ Gran Vía

Bonanno (3, B6) Bonanno is one of the most popular bars in these parts, and draws a good-looking,

arty crowd to its red-hued confines – particularly on Sunday, when the whole affair resembles a sardine can. Which is a good thing (see reference to good-lookers).
☎ 91 366 68 86 ⊠ Plaza del Humilladero 4 ⓥ noon-2am Sun-Thu, to 2.30am Fri & Sat Ⓜ La Latina

Café Belén (4, D6) If the streets surrounding this bar are a little *too* young for you, then relax. You and your grown-up friends can sit and listen to an eclectic selection of music without shouting at each other, all while enjoying excellent cocktails (especially the *mojitos* – rum-based cocktails).
☎ 91 308 27 47 ⊠ Calle de Belén 5 ⓥ 3.30pm-3am Ⓜ Chueca, Alonso Martínez

Café del Círculo de Bellas Artes (3, G3) This cavernous *belle époque* (1919) space is marvellous for a caffeine or champagne hit, or a meal while resting weary feet and sussing out the well-dressed patrons from the terrace. To gain access, you'll need a temporary membership

token (€1). Definitely the best spot to revel in the monumental architecture of the surrounding area.
☎ 91 531 85 03 ⊠ Calle de Alcalá 42 ⓥ 9am-1am Ⓜ Sevilla, Banco de España

Café Matritum (3, B5) One of Madrid's better tiny bars, with excellent music filling the space and attracting a crowd of musicians on nights off. There's a petite mezzanine level and a few seats to hand, but don't be surprised if you're standing for much of the night, chatting to anyone and everyone.
☎ 91 364 01 25 ⊠ Calle del Nuncio 19 ⓥ 3.30pm-3am Wed-Mon Ⓜ La Latina

Cervecería Alemana (3, F5) A definite must-do on the Hemingway pilgrimage. The tapas and beers here attract many tourists at night, but it retains a local feel during the day. The waiters wear bow ties, the tables have marble tops and both can support a good weight of wonderful *calamares*, *tortilla* and *cerveza* (calamari, potato omelette and beer).
☎ 91 429 70 33 ⊠ Plaza de Santa Ana 6 ⓥ 11am-12.30am Sun-Thu, to 2am Fri & Sat Ⓜ Antón Martín, Sol

Del Diego (3, F2) For a bar with a blonde-wood Art-Deco look going on and waiters who appear to have been inspired by the Chris Isaak school of grooming, Del Diego has a fitting list of

Raise your glass to Hemingway at Cervecería Alemana

cocktails and all the grown-up sexiness you'd expect from such a sophisticated tippling spot.
☎ 91 523 31 06 ⊠ Calle de la Reina 12 ⏾ 7pm-3am Mon-Thu, to 3.30am Fri & Sat Ⓜ Gran Vía

Delic (3, B5) Delightful Delic is the best place in town for a leisurely coffee with fabulous tomato-covered toast in the day and some seriously grand *mojitos* at night, when the spunky crowd spills out onto heavenly Plaza de la Paja and all seems right with the world.
☎ 91 364 54 50 ⊠ Plaza de la Paja 8 ⏾ 11am-2am Tue-Sat, to midnight Sun Ⓜ La Latina

El Eucalipto (2, C9) El Eucalipto makes some of the best *mojitos* we've ever had, which is saying something in this cocktail-loving town. The vibe is South American, friendly and chatty, partly because this particular

street has a reputation for a breezy, unpretentious atmosphere, especially when there's outdoor seating in summer.
⊠ Calle de Argumosa 4 ⏾ 6pm-2am Ⓜ Lavapiés

El Viajero (3, B6) The ground floor serves good food, but we prefer to venture upstairs, where the 1st floor offers a bar with great music (dub, acid jazz and funk) and the 2nd floor has our favourite terrace in Madrid, with views of the area's skyline. Get in early for the terrace in summer or book ahead.
☎ 91 366 90 64 ⊠ Plaza de la Cebada 11 ⏾ 1pm-12.30am Tue-Thu & Sun, to 1am Fri & Sat Ⓜ La Latina

Matador Bar (3, E4) Playing good flamenco music, this popular bar has been going for more than 10 years. The bar staff are friendly and swarthy, the crowd vibrant

and the downstairs toilets as scary as ever.
☎ 91 531 89 91 ⊠ Calle de la Cruz 39 ⏾ noon-2am Sun-Thu, to 2.30am Fri & Sat Ⓜ Sol

Museo Chicote (3, F2) A sense of tradition hangs over this Art-Deco bar, a remnant of the 1940s and '50s when this was Madrid's swankiest watering hole, with the likes of Ernest Hemingway and Ava Gardner stopping by. Service is old-school, and so are the cocktails, although you can now hear some great DJs after midnight.
☎ 91 532 67 37 ⊠ Gran Vía 12 ⏾ 7am-3am Mon-Sat Ⓜ Gran Vía

Nuevo Café Barbieri (3, F6) This cavernous old café attracts a mostly young urban crowd. It features damaged walls, velvet curtains, misty mirrors, marble-top tables plus ample opportunities for passive smoking and passionate kissing.
☎ 91 527 36 58 ⊠ Calle del Ave María 45 ⏾ 3pm-2am Sun-Thu, to 3am Fri & Sat Ⓜ Lavapiés

Viva Madrid (3, F4) A damn fine spot for some early-evening tippling and 'a night on the tiles' (the tiles are a famous tourist attraction). It's fine in the late evening too, if you enjoy fighting your way through the heaving crowds, all wanting liquid refreshment.
☎ 91 429 36 40 ⊠ Calle de Manuel Fernández y González 7 ⏾ 1pm-2am Sun-Thu, to 3am Fri & Sat Ⓜ Sevilla, Sol

Wine

The standard accompaniment to many things in Spain, wine comes in three varieties: *tinto* (red), *blanco* (white) and *rosado* (rosé). It can be ordered by the *copa* (glass) or in measures of 500mL or 1L. *Vino de mesa* (table wine) is perfectly decent in most places, but the area around Madrid is not widely regarded as one of Spain's premier wine-producing regions.

RICHARD NEBESKY

DANCE CLUBS

Joy Eslava (3, D3) Going strong for almost 25 years in a building that dates back to 1872, Joy Eslava is something of an institution, and you never know what mix the club's going to attract on any given night, although crowds are a certainty. Everyone here likes the gilt-tinged décor and a guilt-free boogie. Head to Chocolatería de San Ginés (p31) after if you're still going around breakfast time.
☎ 91 366 37 33
✉ Calle del Arenal 11
€ €12-15 ⏱ 11.30pm-5.30am Sun-Thu, to 6am Fri & Sat
Ⓜ Sol

Kapital (2, D8) There are seven, yes, seven floors of nocturnal entertainment here, ranging from dance music, karaoke and galleries to a cinema, with a writhing, sexily clad crowd lapping it all up. Kapital also runs some 'afternoon' sessions for the younger folk. On Sundays it becomes 'Sundance' and draws an up-for-it crowd who have no intention of rolling up to work or university come Monday morning.
☎ 91 420 29 06
✉ Calle de Atocha 125
€ €8 ⏱ early sessions 5.30-11pm Fri, Sat & Sun, late sessions midnight-6am Thu-Sun
Ⓜ Atocha

Ohm (3, D2) A popular night at the Bash Line for those in the mood to

> ### Disco Discounts
> Many of Madrid's streets are littered with brightly coloured cards and fliers by time morning comes around, but it can be a good idea to accept these proffered papers and have a closer look – many offer reduced entry to bars and clubs, and not just the ones that you think must be desperate for some business. Conditions often apply (such as entry before 3am), and please, if you're going to discard a card, use the bin!

'wave your hands in the air like you just don't care' is Ohm (Saturday). Expect a lively mixed (gay and straight) crowd and some of the city's most inclusive, intuitive DJs. Other nights include Bash Line (Wednesday) and house-centric Cream on Thursday.
☎ 91 531 01 32
✉ Plaza del Callao 4
€ €10 ⏱ midnight-6am Tue-Sun Ⓜ Callao

Palacio Gaviria (3, D3) This place really used to be a palace and the luxury trimmings are still evident. People get pretty dressed up, and the queues can be disheartening. Despite its exclusive overtones, it's not frighteningly posh, with 'Exchange' (Thursday – lots of snogging) staking its claim to aiding international relations via house music.
☎ 91 526 60 69
🖳 www.palaciogaviria .com ✉ Calle del Arenal 9 € €9-15
⏱ 11pm-4am Mon-Wed, to 5.30am Thu-Sat, 8.30pm-2am Sun
Ⓜ Sol

Room at Stella (3, F3) The Room is absolutely packed by about 3am, so you'll need to arrive well before then to ensure that you get the chance to dance to one of Madrid's best DJs, Ángel García. A vibrant, heady place, with some great visuals, even if you're almost cross-eyed from partying.
✉ Calle de Arlabán 7
€ €10 ⏱ 1am-6am Fri
Ⓜ Sevilla

Suite (3, F3) There's a restaurant-café here, and it's not a bad 'quiet drink' spot during the day (especially if you still want your surrounds to look stylish), but we like it when things kick-off after midnight on weekends – that's when everyone's shaking out the cobwebs on the dance floor to some seriously funky DJ sounds. A popular spot for gays and straights alike.
☎ 91 521 40 31
✉ Calle de Virgen de los Peligros 4
€ free ⏱ 9pm-2am Mon-Thu, to 3am Fri & Sat Ⓜ Sevilla

CINEMAS

Standard cinema tickets cost around €5.80 (about €6 on weekends), but many cinemas have at least one day set aside as the *día del espectador* (viewer's day) with cut-price tickets (usually at €4). You can purchase tickets at the cinemas or in advance (in some cases) on ☎ 90 222 91 22 or online at www.guiadelocio.com (in Spanish).

Alphaville (2, B6) Come here to avoid mainstream foreign fare and mix it with a few arty types, as it shows original-language films with a more independent streak than other cinemas in Madrid. There are four screens, and three theatres have wheelchair access. ☎ 91 559 38 36 ✉ Calle de Martín de los Heros 14 € €5.80, Mon €3.80 ⌚ from 4.30pm Ⓜ Plaza de España ♿ good

Cine Doré (3, F6) The Cine Doré is a delightful old cinema, housing the Filmoteca Nacional (national film library), and you can expect to see classics old and new, in their original languages. There's also a library and bar-restaurant attached. ☎ 91 549 00 11 ✉ Calle de Santa Isabel 3 € €1.35, 10-ticket pass €10.20 ⌚ 5.30pm Ⓜ Antón Martín

Renoir Plaza de España (2, B7) This is part of a chain of cinemas that all specialise in original-language films (there is another at Calle de Princesa 5). The theatres all have excellent facilities and you can prebook your tickets on the web, as outlined above. ☎ 91 541 41 00 ✉ Calle de Martín de los Heros 12 € €5.80/4 ⌚ from 4pm Ⓜ Plaza de España ♿

LIVE MUSIC VENUES

Café Central (3, E5) This is probably Madrid's best place to hear live jazz centrally, with both local and international acts deigning to play here. The atmosphere's good too – you're close to the stage without feeling as though you're in a broom closet, and there's an intimate, low-key vibe. ☎ 91 369 41 43 🖥 www.cafecentral madrid.com in Spanish ✉ Plaza de Ángel 10 € about €12 ⌚ 1.30pm-2.30am Sun-Thu, to 3.30am Fri & Sat Ⓜ Sol, Antón Martín

Café Populart (3, F5) A small and intimate yet lively venue with a tiny stage and some pretty smart service. You can enjoy blues, jazz, Cuban, reggae, flamenco and swing here. ☎ 91 429 84 07 🖥 www .populart.es in Spanish ✉ Calle de las Huertas 22 € free ⌚ 6pm-2.30am Mon-Thu, to 3.30am Fri & Sat, shows at 11pm Ⓜ Antón Martín

Calle 54 (4, E1) Offering soul-satisfying Latin jazz, this is a great place to hear great live music. Partly owned by filmmaker Fernando Trueba, whose movie *Calle 54* was its inspiration, it's an upscale place that attracts musicians, film stars and locals. Live shows start around 11pm. ☎ 90 214 14 12 ✉ Paseo de la Habana 3 € about €15 ⌚ 1pm-late Ⓜ Nuevos Ministerios, Santiago Bernabéu

Clamores (4, C5) Clamores gets a well-regarded selection of jazz artists to play. Another bonus is a little freedom of movement that comes with the non-*centro* premises and the mix of other music styles, such as Brazilian or flamenco. ☎ 91 445 79 38 ✉ Calle de Alburquerque 14

Calle 54; the next best thing to being in a real movie

RICHARD NEBESKY

€ around €10 ⏰ 6pm-3am Sun-Thu, to 4am Fri & Sat Ⓜ Bilbao

El Sol (3, E3) Independent bands (local and foreign) get a live airing here before the funk takes over, and it's a bit of a haven for those who want a slightly grungier, crimson-lit atmosphere. Not as important as it was in the 1980s *movida* scene, but still very lively.
☎ 91 532 64 90 ✉ Calle de los Jardines 3 € €10 ⏰ concerts from

11.30pm, 12.30am-5am Tue-Sat Ⓜ Gran Vía

Galileo Galilei (4, A3) Enthusiasts of live Latin music will enjoy a visit here. The music dominates your attention, but there are also magic shows and comedy gigs at times. It's a good space too, with room to breathe and to move (should the mood take you).
☎ 91 534 75 57 🖳 www.salagalileo galilei.com in Spanish

✉ Calle de Galileo 100 € around €10 ⏰ 6pm-4.30am Ⓜ Canal

Honky Tonk (4, D5) Despite the name, this is a great place to see local rock 'n' roll, though many acts have a little country thrown in the mix too. A very diverse crowd packs into this smallish club; arrive early as the place fills up fast.
☎ 91 445 68 86 ✉ Calle de Covarrubias 24 ⏰ 9.30pm-5.30am Ⓜ Alonso Martínez

FLAMENCO

Café de Chinitas (3, B2) This is a cut above many flamenco joints, but you'll need to book to dine and enjoy the shows here. Famous past audience members include Bill Clinton and the king of Spain, and the performers are often well known too.
☎ 91 559 51 35 🖳 www.chinitas.com ✉ Calle de Torija 7 € €35 ⏰ 9pm-2.30am Mon-Sat, show 10.30pm Ⓜ Santo Domingo

Cardamomo (3, F4) Many locals with a love of flamenco were thrilled when this place opened in

2002. Flamenco jam sessions take place Wednesday at 10.30pm, and there's always good music on offer even if you miss one of these. It's a dark, stylish and sexy place – the perfect background for the good-looking patrons, staff and performers.
☎ 91 369 07 57 🖳 www.cardamomo .net in Spanish ✉ Calle Echegaray 15 € free ⏰ 9pm-3am Ⓜ Sevilla

Casa Patas (3, E5) This is an excellent and comfortable space in which to enjoy recognised masters of flamenco guitar, song

and dance. Famous faces can often be found both on stage and in the crowd, and you'd do well to book in advance. Courses in flamenco can also be organised and good food is available.
☎ 91 369 04 96 🖳 www.casapatas.com ✉ Calle de Cañizares 10 € about €30 ⏰ noon-5pm & 8pm-3am, shows 10.30pm Mon-Thu, 9pm & midnight Fri & Sat Ⓜ Antón Martín

Corral de la Morería (3, A5) This is another dinner-and-a-show *tablao* (tourist-oriented flamenco), but this one is actually worth considering. It's not as big and flash as some of the others, and the quality's good so you won't feel as though you've just been caught in a tourist trap.
☎ 91 365 84 46 🖳 www.corraldela moreria.com ✉ Calle de la Morería 17 € from €32 ⏰ 9pm-2am, show at 10.30pm Ⓜ La Latina

Duende
Duende is the heart and soul of flamenco, but trying to come up with a definitive description of it is no mean feat. It's that moment when a performer seems to disappear into their art. It's what poet García Lorca described as 'black sounds'. The best way we can think of recognising it is when the hairs on the back of your neck stand up, your eyes are pricked with tears, a shiver goes down your spine and the locals are all calling out 'Olé!'.

CLASSICAL MUSIC, OPERA, DANCE & THEATRE

Auditorio Nacional de Música (2, E4) Don't let the hideously ugly exterior put you off too much. The inside is more than comfortable and, most importantly if you're listening to music, it's great for acoustics. This auditorium is also the home of La Orquestra y Coro Nacionales de España (Spain's national orchestra), which means you can feast on classical music from October to June.
☎ 91 337 03 07
🖳 www.auditorio nacional.mcu.es ✉ Calle del Príncipe de Vergara 146 € varies box office 4-6pm Mon, 10am-5pm Tue-Fri, 11am-1pm Sat Ⓜ Cruz del Rayo educational concerts

Centro Cultural de la Villa (4, E6) If you're having trouble finding this theatre, look under the waterfall at Plaza de Colón. You'll find performances of classical music, comic theatre, flamenco, exhibitions, as well as stuff that'll please

Theatre fanatics queue for the latest at Teatro Español

the kids, in this 800-plus capacity venue.
☎ 91 575 60 80
✉ Plaza de Colón box office 11am-1.30pm & 5-6pm Tue-Sun € varies Ⓜ Colón kids' theatre

Teatro Albéniz (3, E4) A variety of performances are staged here, from opera and *zarzuela* (Spanish light opera) to plays and dance (including flamenco). If you're here in August, don't miss the chance to see Alicia Alonso's Ballet Nacional de Cuba annual performance of the ballet classics.
☎ 91 531 83 11 ✉ Calle de la Paz 11 € varies box office 11.30am-1pm & 5.30-9pm Ⓜ Sol

Teatro Español (3, F4) A theatre has stood on this spot since 1583. Known as the Teatro Español since 1849, the theatre's repertoire consists mostly of contemporary Spanish drama and some gems from the 17th century. It's a beautiful theatre, and worth a visit even if you understand nothing of what's being said.
☎ 91 360 14 84 ✉ Calle del Príncipe 25 € varies box office 11.30am-1.30pm & 5-7pm Ⓜ Sol, Sevilla

Teatro Real (3, B3) The grandest stage in the city and one of the world's most technically advanced theatres. Acoustics are superb, seats are comfy and at intermission you can enjoy lovely views over Plaza de Oriente and the Palacio Real. Catch opera, ballet, classical music and flamenco (July) performances here. Tickets can be bought on the website.
☎ 91 516 06 06
🖳 www.teatro-real.com in Spanish ✉ Plaza de Oriente € varies box office 10am-1.30pm & 5.30-8pm Mon-Sat Ⓜ Ópera matinees

La Casa Encendida

One of the most exciting community projects to happen in Madrid in recent times has been the creation of **La Casa Encendida** (2, C9; ☎ 91 506 38 75; www .lacasaencendida.com in Spanish; Ronda de Valencia 2; 10am-10pm; Ⓜ Embajadores) – a mammoth arts centre that houses gallery and performances spaces and also hosts language classes and other community initiatives. Tickets for events as diverse as sound-art performances, plays, modern dance pieces and screenings of rare foreign films happen on a very regular basis and at cheap prices (around €3).

GAY & LESBIAN MADRID

Café Aquarela (3, G1) The décor here is part colonial gentlemen's club and part opium den. This smallish bar is great to replenish a thirst after a hard day or to start the mood before a big night. The crowd? Think lesbians on first dates, gay men on last dates, and everything in between.
☎ 91 522 21 43 ✉ Calle de Gravina 10 ⏱ 11am-2am Sun-Thu, to 3am Fri & Sat Ⓜ Chueca

Medea (3, F6) Madrid's gay scene is famously open to all, but for those nights when it's the sisterhood or nothing, you can try Medea. This girl-friendly establishment has good music and a pool table, and none of Chueca's madness.
✉ Calle de la Cabeza 33 ⏱ 11pm-5am Thu-Sat Ⓜ Antón Martín

Rick's (3, F2) Sooner or later, everyone comes to Rick's. It's not that it's a particularly great place, it's just that it's a bit of an institution that's popular with local and out-of-town gays (mostly men). Look

> ### Gay Pride
> Madrid's gay and lesbian pride festival and parade take place on the last Saturday in June each year. It's known as the *Día del Orgullo de Gays, Lesbians y Transexuales* and the partying is intense, intrepid and inspiring.

for the purple and black exterior and dive right in, if you can find space.
✉ Calle de Clavel 8 ⏱ 11pm-late Ⓜ Gran Vía

Shangay Tea Dance (3, C2) Even the toilets are the last word in style here. Cool Ballroom hosts the Shangay Tea Dance every Sunday. The incredibly good-looking crowd is often entertainment in itself, but the DJs deserve a special mention for dishing up house music that gets you right where you live. On other nights, it's fashionably hard to get into if you're not a handsome gay man with his good-looking fag hag.
☎ 91 542 34 39 🖥 www.coolballroom .com ✉ Calle de Isabel la Católica 6 € €8

⏱ 9pm-2am Sun Ⓜ Santo Domingo

Strong Center (3, C3) Time to toughen up and get the leather out! For hombres only, this place is not for the faint-hearted or faint-cocked. The dark room is famous, or infamous, depending on who you're talking to, and generally full.
☎ 91 541 54 15 ✉ Calle de Trujillo 7 € €8 ⏱ midnight-6am Ⓜ Callao

Sunrise (3, F2) With its bright red walls and perky pop music, this mainly gay spot isn't for serious clubbers, but it's a fun and friendly place to dance or meet new people.
☎ 91 522 43 17 ✉ Calle de Barbieri 7 ⏱ 10pm-3.30am Thu, midnight-6am Fri & Sat Ⓜ Chueca

SPECTATOR SPORTS

See the Tickets & Listings section (p59) for details of buying tickets.

Athletics
On the last Sunday in April, the **Maratón Popular de Madrid** (a marathon) is held. You can get information at www.maratonmadrid.org.

Bullfighting
You've got to admit, any life-and-death sport that involves donning pink silk socks and a skin-tight sequined suit is going to be interesting.

Worth seeing is the **Feria de San Isidro** (Festival of San Isidro), which takes place from mid-May and lasts into June. Tickets for this can be hard to come by though. Regular *corridas* (fights) take place from March to October, generally on Sunday at 7pm. Bullfights take place at the beautiful, enormous **Plaza de Toros Monumental de Las Ventas** (p29). Tickets cost from about €4 for a spot in the sun *(sol)* to €120 for a spot in the shade *(sombra)*, and can be purchased at the **ticket office** (⌚ 10am-2pm & 5-8pm Fri-Sun) at the ring or by phoning ☎ 91 356 22 00.

Head to Plaza de Toros for pink silk socks, sequinned suits, and life-and-death battles

Cycling

La Vuelta de España (Tour of Spain) finishes its spoke-fest in Madrid (having started three weeks before in Valencia) on the second-last Sunday of September. For details, visit www.lavuelta.com.

Football

The biggest spectator sport in Madrid is, of course, football. Madrid's most glamorous team is Real Madrid, which plays at **Estadio Santiago Bernabéu** (p31). Other teams are Atlético de Madrid, which plays at **Estadio Vicente Calderón** (2, A9; ☎ 91 366 47 07; www.at-madrid.com in Spanish; Calle de la Virgen del Puerto; Ⓜ Pirámides); and Rayo Vallecano, which plays at **Nuevo Estadio de Vallecas Teresa Rivero** (☎ 91 478 22 53; www.rayovallecano.es in Spanish; Avenida del Payaso Fofó, Vallecas; Ⓜ Portazgo) – the latter has a reputation for a jovial atmosphere at their games, unlike the other two, whose games are fairly serious events. Tickets for a Real Madrid match will cost from €10 and can change hands (illegally) for thousands, but they can be hard to come by for important matches. Tickets can be bought from stadiums, ticket offices around the city or by phone on ☎ 90 232 43 24.

Tennis

Madrid now plays host to the **Tennis Masters series** (which attracts big bucks and bigger names) in October. A 9000-seat indoor hard court, **Madrid Arena** (☎ 90 218 36 47; Calle de las Aves; Ⓜ Lago) hosts the event in Casa de Campo. For more information go to www.tennis-masters-madrid.com.

Sleeping

Madrid has excellent accommodation in every price bracket, but it can be wise to book ahead, as capital status makes her a very popular place for business travellers and tourists alike.

The city has many highly regarded jaw-dropping deluxe hotels that will have you wanting to move in permanently. Styles vary between state-of-the-art minimalist lodgings to old-world five-star palaces slathered in gilt and laden with chandeliers. Every possible amenity you can think of is on offer, from pillow menus (literally a menu of pillows for you to choose from) to Internet-email access in every room, or luxury restaurants and whatever-your-heart-desires room service. Madrid's top-end hotels can be good places to score special weekend or 'corporate' rates, as are midrange places, with quieter periods seeing prices drop. You can often find nonsmoking sections in such hotels, plus business facilities and places to eat. Madrid's budget hotels are often in the noisier parts of town, with simple but spotless rooms (all places to stay mentioned in this chapter have en suite facilities) and welcoming management.

> ### Room Rates
> The prices in this chapter indicate the cost per night of a standard double room and are intended as a guide only. The reviews assess the character and facilities of each place within the context of the price bracket.
>
> | | |
> | --- | --- |
> | Deluxe | over €250 |
> | Top End | €150–249 |
> | Midrange | €75–149 |
> | Budget | under €74 |

Accommodation comes in two categories: hotels (H), and *hostales* (Hs; cheap to midrange hotels), with signs indicating each place's status. All hotels are subject to the 7% value-added tax known as IVA.

Beware: check into a deluxe Madrid hotel, such as Hotel Ritz, and you may never want to leave

DELUXE

Hesperia Madrid (4, E3)
When a hotel's list of attributes includes a beautiful interior courtyard, one of the city's greatest restaurants and a piano bar with 'Madrid's widest selection of whiskies', then you hardly have to worry about an unpleasant surprise. Everything is better than good here – from the service to the design (handled by Pasqua Ortega, who remodelled the Teatro Real).
☎ 91 210 88 00 ☐ www .hesperia-madrid.com ✉ Paseo de la Castellana 57 Ⓜ Gregorio Marañón, Nuevos Ministerios ♿ fair ✖ Santceloni (p58) ♿

Hotel AC Santo Mauro (4, D5) Sigh. A truly stunning hotel. We were seriously tempted to move into the Santo Mauro (named after the palace's former owner, the Marquis de Santo Mauro) when were shown the tasteful rooms, beautifully renovated common areas, an indoor swimming pool and a delightful garden area where late suppers are served. You can see how Posh and Becks managed to run up a bill in the hundreds of thousands over many months spent revelling in the luxury here.
☎ 91 319 69 00 ☐ www.ac-hoteles.com ✉ Calle de Zurbano 36 Ⓜ Rubén Darío, Alonso Martínez ✖ Faisandé ♿

Hotel Orfila (4, D6) The former home of the exiled Queen of Bulgaria, this

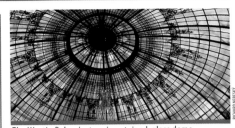
The Westin Palace's stunning stained-glass dome

RICHARD NEBESKY

charming 19th-century palace is one of Madrid's best places to rest one's glamorous head. Antique furnishings from the 18th and 19th centuries fill the rooms and common areas, and staff seems capable of anticipating your every need before you even feel it.
☎ 91 702 77 72 ☐ www.hotelorfila.com ✉ Calle de Orfila 6 Ⓜ Alonso Martínez

✖ El Jardín de Orfila

Hotel Ritz (3, H4) The Ritz opened its doors in 1920 under the watchful eye of both King Alfonso XIII and Cesar Ritz, and there's no chance of standards slipping as it approaches 100 years of ritziness. Even the sheets (hand-embroidered) are luxurious; business and fitness facilities are uniformly excellent and its previous reputation for ferocious snootiness has softened.
☎ 91 701 67 67 ☐ www.ritzmadrid.com ✉ Plaza de la Lealtad 5 Ⓜ Banco de España ♿ good ✖ Goya ♿

Hotel Villa Real (3, G4) Salivating, we decided that this was the place to stay if

you wanted to absorb both art's Golden Triangle and the nightlife of Huertas and Santa Ana. Service is bend-over-backwards gracious, with everything you could hope for, all provided in an enchanting, art-filled setting that manages to avoid the clichés.
☎ 91 420 37 67 ☐ www.derbyhotels.es ✉ Plaza de las Cortes 10 Ⓜ Banco de España ♿ good ✖ East 47 (p51) ♿

Westin Palace (3, H4)
Commissioned by none other than King Alfonso XIII himself (who wanted a comfortable place for his wedding guests to stay), this elegant hotel, built in 1910 on the site of the former palace of the Duque de Lerma, has not let up on the luxury since. No detail has been overlooked, and we love the stunning stained-glass dome, the fancy bathrooms and the sheer 'marblelousness' of the 465-room palace.
☎ 91 360 80 00 ☐ www .westin.com ✉ Plaza de las Cortes 7 Ⓜ Banco de España ♿ good ✖ La Rotonda ♿

TOP END

Bauzá (2, E7) Hotel Bauzá opened in 1999 and revels in its own modern, minimalist beauty. Everything is stunning here, with not an inch of chintz or a hint of ruffle. Rooms are beautifully decorated, airy and reasonably spacious, and include lots of little luxuries, such as a pillow menu.
☎ 91 435 75 45 💻 www.hotelbauza.com ✉ Calle de Goya 79 Ⓜ Goya ✕ Bauzá ⚲

Catalonia Moratín (3, E5) Housed in a nicely restored, 18th-century palace, this is a great, swanky place to stay, but is surprisingly located on the at times gritty Calle de Atocha. The original stone entryway is very impressive, but even better is the bright interior patio beyond it. Rooms are capacious and chic, with hardwood floors and balconies for every room.
☎ 91 369 71 71 💻 www.hoteles-catalonia.es ✉ Calle de Atocha 23 Ⓜ Antón Martín ♿ limited ✕ restaurant ⚲

Hotel Alcalá (2, E7) Despite its size, this hotel retains quite an intimate atmosphere, with kind staff at the front desk and some unusual touches, such as seven suites with decorative touches designed by *movida*-queen-turned-fashion-designer Agatha Ruiz de la Prada. The other rooms are perfectly comfortable and stylish,
and popular with business travellers.
☎ 91 435 10 60 💻 www.nh-hoteles.es ✉ Calle de Alcalá 66 Ⓜ Príncipe de Vergara ✕ restaurant & café ⚲

Hotel Intur Palacio San Martín (3, D3) Set on a picturesque plaza in the former US embassy, this beautiful (and beautifully run) hotel offers elegant luxury without going overboard. Rooms are light-filled, spacious and sunny, with enormous beds. Room 103 is especially large, if you like stretching out.
☎ 91 701 50 00 💻 www.intur.com ✉ Plaza de San Martín 5 Ⓜ Callao ✕ restaurant ⚲

Hotel Suecia (3, G3) They say: 'We just want to be the nicest' – and they *are* extremely nice here, with
high standards (particularly good for business travellers), comfortably elegant rooms and extra points for being able to boast that Hemingway stayed here in the 1950s.
☎ 91 531 69 00 💻 www.hotelsuecia.com ✉ Calle Marqués de Casa Riera 4 Ⓜ Banco de España ✕ Beliman ⚲

Quo (3, F3) Oozing a certain NYC sensibility (without the attitude), the Quo is a wonderful choice for those wishing to stay close to the action but who enjoy a feeling of individuality with their décor. Black-clad staff attend to every whim with aplomb, and the simple-but-elegant design staples and luxuries offer an escape from the bustle outside.
☎ 91 532 90 49 💻 www.hotelesquo.com ✉ Calle de Sevilla 4 Ⓜ Sevilla

Breakfast Included

Many Madrileños aren't big on breakfast, with a coffee and a pastry deemed a sufficient way to start the day. This is one reason to avoid paying exorbitant rates (say, €15) for hotel breakfasts served by a certain hour. Even if they are included in the room rates, they're generally pretty desultory affairs, and not worth the effort. Get outside and go to a café instead.

RICHARD NEBESKY

MIDRANGE

Hotel II Castillas (3, D3)
This newish central hotel has casual rooms on the diminutive side, but they have hardwood floors and a pretty beige-and-blue colour motif. The bathrooms have perks such as heated towel racks and a make-up mirror. The staff is helpful with sightseeing arrangements.
☎ 91 524 97 50
🖳 www.hoteldoscastillas.com ✉ Calle de la Abada 7 Ⓜ Sol
✕ restaurant

Hotel Cliper (3, E2) Part of the High Tech hotels chain, the Cliper offers some great perks, such as a free ADSL line in all rooms, computers available for guest use and hydro-massage showers, plus an exercise bike for your own use. Rooms are stylish, done in neutral colours, and some top-end rooms even come with their own PC.
☎ 91 531 17 00
🖳 www.hthotels.com

The view from Hotel Miau looks better than it sounds

RICHARD NEBESKY

Children & Hospitality

Apart from top-end and deluxe places, which cater to every whim, Madrid's hotels don't go overboard with family-friendly details. There are often many flights of stairs (or tiny elevators with no room for a pram) and the nightlife outside is generally unmuffled. You can ask for children's cots, and they'll be provided in some places, but it's best to look for the 🚼 in our reviews.

✉ Calle Chinchilla 6
Ⓜ Santo Domingo
♿ limited

Hotel HH Campomanes (3, C3) A stylish and very modern addition to Madrid's hotel scene, the Campomanes has a black-and-white décor and a subdued coolness to all of its 30 rooms, although service is not as 'jump to it' as you might expect. A very slick package all round though, and in a prime location for sightseeing.
☎ 91 548 85 48
🖳 www.hhcampomanes.com ✉ Calle de Campomanes 4 Ⓜ Ópera
♿ limited 🚼

Hotel Miau (3, F5) If you want to be close to the nightlife of Plaza de Santa Ana, then this is the place for you. Opened in 2002, a genuine effort has been made (with success) to offer a smart, stylish alternative to some of the scruffier places in the area. Still, it's a noisy district, so you'll want to pack earplugs if you've scored a balcony room.
☎ 91 369 71 20
🖳 www.hotelmiau.com

✉ Calle del Príncipe 26
Ⓜ Antón Martín
✕ restaurant-bar

Hotel París (3, E4) With just a touch of faded grandeur, this hotel, smack-bang on the Plaza de la Puerta del Sol and under the famous Tío Pepe sign, is a good choice in this area. Rooms have TV, phone, air-con and a lot of fabric details, and the staff are helpful.
☎ 91 521 54 91
✉ Calle de Alcalá 2
Ⓜ Sol

Hotel Preciados (3, C2) Near Plaza de la Puerta de Sol, this stylish hotel has very comfortable, soundproofed rooms with all amenities (even a free minibar) and a pretty, historic façade. This is the sort of place we get letters about — for all the right reasons. Parking can also be arranged and there's a floor devoted to female business travellers.
☎ 91 454 44 00
🖳 www.preciadoshotel.com ✉ Calle de Preciados 37 Ⓜ Callao, Sol, Santo Domingo
✕ Café Varela

BUDGET

Hostal Dulcinea (3, G5)
In a location close to Plaza de Santa Ana, but with some rooms quiet enough to let you get some shut-eye (others are a little noisy), the spotlessly clean Dulcinea is a strong choice in this range. The owners are courteous and helpful; if it's full they can direct you to their other property across the street.
☎ 91 429 93 09
🖳 donato@teleline.es
✉ Calle de Cervantes 19, Level 2 Ⓜ Antón Martín

Hostal la Macarena
(3, C4) Housed in a well-groomed building on the western side of Plaza Mayor, this efficient, safe place offers smallish, quiet rooms, with TV and air-con, plus a hard-to-beat position for those who love this part of town.
☎ 91 365 92 21 ✉ Cava de San Miguel 8 Ⓜ Sol

Hostal la Zona (3, E2)
La Zona has a loyal gay following and combines great proximity to the city's pinkest barrio with decent décor, sassy (but helpful service) and a cheery atmosphere. Try and score

room No 203 – with a sunny balcony.
☎ 91 521 99 04
🖳 www.hostallazona.com ✉ Calle de Valverde 7, Level 1 Ⓜ Gran Vía

Hostal Madrid (3, D4)
A real find in this category, the Madrid has with-it management who are really helpful, while the rooms (fewer than 20) are a definite cut above the usual (although ones in the building's interior are a little dark), with TV, air-con, phone, hairdryer and safe. You can also self-cater in their miniapartments, although the proximity to restaurants might put paid to that.
☎ 91 522 00 60 🖳 www.hostal-madrid.info
✉ Calle de Esparteros 6 Ⓜ Sol

Hostal Maria Cristina
(3, F1) After the hustle of Calle de Fuencarral and a flight of stairs, the lobby – which resembles your grandma's living room in the 1970s – is quite comforting. Creaky parquet floors and a busy-bee approach to cleanliness only reinforce the feeling. Rooms

GUY MOBERLY

are simple and bathrooms sparkle.
☎ 91 531 63 00
🖳 www.iespana.es /hostalmariacristina
✉ Calle de Fuencarral 20 Ⓜ Gran Vía ⓗ

Hostal San Lorenzo
(3, F2) Close to the action of Chueca but not in the thick of it, this friendly and charming hotel is like a quiet escape from the world outside. The original stone walls of this 19th-century building have been left exposed, adding character you won't find elsewhere, and rooms have excellent new bathrooms and an easy, attractive style.
☎ 91 521 30 57
🖳 www.hostal-lorenzo.com ✉ Calle de Clavel 8, Level 1 Ⓜ Gran Vía ⓗ

Those Precious Zzzzzs
You'll wonder if anyone sleeps in Madrid, and may well go way past your bedtime most nights, but if you're counting on some real shut-eye, it might be wise to avoid hotel rooms that face the street in Madrid's nightlife barrios (neighbourhoods). When you add the noise of revelry to the late-night garbage collection, early-morning street cleaning and roadworks, sirens, church bells, barking dogs, howling kids and arguing couples, you get quite a decibel cocktail. Light sleepers beware! Deluxe and top-end hotels will be more familiar with double-glazing on windows than will midrange and budget hotels.

About Madrid

HISTORY

Muslim Influence

Magerit, or Mayrit, as it came to be known, was a fortified Muslim garrison against the small Christian kingdoms to the north from 854 until well into the 10th century. Very little evidence of this period survives, although the area between La Latina and the Palacio Real is still known as the *morería,* or Moorish quarter. Magerit was handed over to Christian rule in 1085 in exchange for the preferred area of Valencia.

Royals vs Reality

The royal court sat in Madrid for the first time in 1309, but it wasn't until 1561 that Madrid became the capital of Spain. The place still had unpaved lanes and filthy alleys, and suffered in comparison to other cities of Europe. It had no navigable river or substantial port, and trade and communications with the rest of the country were difficult. The royal court spent untold sums on its sumptuous existence in an attempt to retreat from the squalid reality that surrounded it. The population swelled with immigrants hoping to gain patronage or a post with the machinery of government.

The mid-1700s were marked by a change in the ruling dynasty and resulted in a period of common-sense government, with Carlos III at the helm. Madrid was generally cleaned up and attention turned to public works (with the completion of the Palacio Real and inauguration of the Jardín Botánico) and a fostering of the intellectual life of the city.

Napoleonic Interlude

Around 1805 France and Spain conspired to take Portugal. By 1808 the resulting French presence had become an occupation and Napoleon's brother was crowned king.

On 2 May 1808 townspeople attacked French troops around the Palacio Real and what is now Plaza del Dos de Mayo. The rebels were soundly

---

11 March 2004

In the rush hour of 11 March 2004, 10 separate bombs went off on three commuter trains heading into Madrid's Atocha station, killing 191 people and wounding 1400. It was the biggest such terror attack in the nation's history and left the city reeling.

At first it was assumed that the Basque terror group ETA was responsible, and so the ruling right-wing Partido Popular government insisted in the following days. That insistence began to ring hollow as evidence mounted that the attack might have come from a radical Islamic group in reprisal for the government's unswerving support of US President George W Bush's invasion of Iraq. Rather than talk of vengeance and retaliation, the country went to the polls and ousted the government, after massive protests across the country and especially in Madrid.

defeated, but it marked the beginning of the War of Independence, a long campaign to oust the French. In 1812, 30,000 Madrileños perished from hunger alone. By 1813, with help from the British and Portuguese, the war had ended.

A Republic or Civil War?

The first attempt at a republic came in 1873; however, the army had other ideas, and restored the monarchy. A period of relative stability ensued and it wasn't until 1931 that a second republic was called.

By 1931 the rise of Madrid's socialists, and of anarchists elsewhere in Spain, sharpened social tensions. A coalition of republicans and socialists proclaimed the second republic, which led to some reforms and political confrontation. Street violence and divisions within the left helped a right-wing coalition to power in 1933. Then, in 1936, it was the left-wing Frente Popular's turn to be in power. A violent face-off appeared to be inevitable – either the right-wing army would stage a coup, or the left would have its revolution.

The army moved first, and three years of bloody, horrendous warfare ensued. Franco's troops advanced from the south and were in the Casa de Campo (p26) by early November 1936. The government fled, but a hastily assembled mix of recruits, sympathisers and International Brigades held firm, with fighting heaviest in the city's northwest. A battered Madrid finally fell to Franco on 28 March 1939.

The Franco Era

In the dark years of Franco's dictatorship, with Western Europe at war, the right-wing Falangist party maintained a heavy-handed repression, at its harshest in the 1940s. Thousands of people suspected of sympathising with the left were harassed, imprisoned and subjected to forced labour.

Spain was internationally isolated, which lead to the *años de hambre* (years of hunger). Only in 1955 did the average wage again reach the level it had been in 1934. By this time, discontent was expressed in the universities and workers' organisations.

The Cold War saw the US grant economic aid to Franco's Spain in exchange for the use of Spanish air and naval bases. An economic boom followed in the 1960s, but clandestine opposition to Franco's rule remained.

Return to Democracy

When Franco died in 1975, trade union and opposition groups emerged from hiding. By 1977 these groups were legalised and elections were held. A centre-right coalition won power, and set about writing a new constitution in collaboration with the opposition. The constitution provided for a parliamentary monarchy with no state religion and guaranteed a degree of devolution of power to the 17 regions into which the country is now divided.

GOVERNMENT & POLITICS

Three governments rule from Madrid. The national government sits in the Cortes (parliament), divided into the Congreso de los Diputados (lower house) on Carrera de San Jerónimo and the Senado (senate) on Plaza de España.

Madrid province became a separate autonomous region in 1983, governed by a council *(consejo gobierno)*, whose actions are controlled by the regional parliament (Asamblea de Madrid). The country's first-ever woman regional president, the right-wing Esperanza Aguirre, emerged victorious (just) in the last elections. Her undisguised dislike of party fellow Alberto Ruiz-Gallardón promises to add spice to the political landscape. The right-wing Partido Popular's glee was darkened by the bomb attacks (p74) and subsequent victory of the Socialist Party (PSOE) in the country's general elections.

The city government, or *ayuntamiento,* is led by the mayor *(alcalde)* – in May 2003 both the city and the surrounding region (the Comunidad de Madrid) went to the polls. The Madrileños elected the popular former president of the Comunidad, Ruiz-Gallardón, as their mayor.

For administrative purposes, Madrid is divided into 21 districts, each with its own local council *(junta municipal)*.

> **Sounding Off**
> Noise pollution is a chronic problem for Madrid's citizens and visitors. Traffic, late-night partying and rubbish collection, sirens, loud conversations across inner courtyards in apartment blocks and barking dogs all assault the ears. Despite numerous protests by residents in town (look for the banners hanging off apartment balconies near the 'party plazas'), Madrileños are frequently subjected to noise levels of around 80 decibels or more.

ECONOMY

Madrid and its surrounding region are home to a big range of farming and industrial activities. Crops of wheat, barley, corn, potatoes, garlic and grapes (among others), plus livestock, boost agriculture. Principal industries include metallurgy, chemicals, textiles, tobacco, paper and some foodstuffs.

As the Spanish capital, Madrid itself is largely given over to services and big business. It's worth keeping in mind that Madrid was slow to develop during what was for many other cities the Industrial Revolution, and only really developed a middle class from the 1830s onwards. Eternal rival Barcelona has watched with dismay as Madrid has appeared to grow in stature and become the prime financial and economic mover of Spain, shedding its previous image as a bureaucratic deadweight.

Although unemployment fell steeply in the second half of the 1990s, it started to rise again in the new millennium, and rising house prices are forcing the average Madrileño family to spend around 60% of its income on housing.

SOCIETY & CULTURE

Madrid receives huge numbers of tourists every year, but it doesn't seem to phase the locals one bit. You'll find many people who speak English, particularly in the hotel and restaurant trade, but even a smattering of Spanish (officially known as *castellano*) will be patiently and warmly received, so learn a few basic phrases and don't be shy.

About 300,000 migrants live in the city: Ecuadorians, Colombians and Moroccans comprise the majority, with Pakistanis, Africans, Chinese and Latin Americans filling the ranks. Many 'Madrileños' also hail from elsewhere in Spain, making for a lively mix of cultures and accents.

Most Madrileños profess to be Catholic, although this is often little more than lip service on a day-to-day basis. Still, passion remains strong for Easter processions and local fiestas for patron saints.

> **Did You Know?**
> - Madrid's population is 3.1 million
> - The average annual salary in Madrid is €19,650
> - Madrid is the highest capital city in Europe at 650.7m above sea level

GUY MOBERLY

Etiquette

Madrileños can be economical with etiquette such as *'por favor'* (please) and *'gracias'* (thank you), but don't take this as a sign of rudeness. That said, it's customary when in a bar or small shop to wish everyone a hearty *'buenas días'* (good day) when you enter and *'adiós'* (goodbye) when you leave. It's perfectly acceptable to attract the attention of the waiter or barstaff with *'oigo'* (literally, 'hear me') and the norm to respond to thanks with *'de nada'* (it's nothing). The standard form of greeting between men and women is a light kiss on each cheek, from right to left. Men seem to take or leave handshakes on informal occasions, but they're pretty much standard in a business context. Women who are meeting for the first time – except in business situations – will generally kiss each cheek.

The Spanish concept of time is more relaxed than that of some other countries, but things that need a fixed time get one and it's generally adhered to. Littering is the norm, and in bars it's generally perfectly acceptable to chuck paper, toothpicks, cigarette butts etc onto the floor, but it's best to suss out what others are doing first.

Born & Bred
True-blue, dyed-in-the-wool Madrileños are known as *castizos* or *chulapos* (generally abbreviated to *chulos* – although the word can have some negative connotations, so perhaps it's best not to bandy it about). Occasionally you'll hear working-class men and women of Lavapiés referred to as *manolos* and *manolas* respectively, a reference to the popularity of the names Manolo and Manola.

ARTS
Architecture

Madrid is bereft of signs of the earlier stages of Spain's architectural history. Only a stretch of wall remains to indicate Madrid's status as an early Muslim outpost, and the bell towers of the Iglesia de San Pedro El Viejo (p25) and Iglesia de San Nicolás de los Servitas (p25) are the only survivors of the Mudéjar style, which features a preponderance of brickwork. The much-interfered-with Casa de los Lujanes (p17) is the sole example of late-Gothic architecture.

Juan de Herrera (1530–97) was the greatest figure of the Spanish Renaissance, and he developed a style that bears almost no resemblance to anything else of the period. His great masterpiece was the palace-monastery complex of San Lorenzo de El Escorial (p36). Even after his death, Herrera's style lived on in Madrid. Termed *barroco madrileño* (Madrid baroque), his stern style is fused with a restrained approach to the voluptuous ornamentation inherent in the baroque period. Buildings that fall into this category include the Real Casa de la Panadería (p14), the Catedral de San Isidro (p24), the *ayuntamiento* (town hall; p17) and the Convento de la Encarnación (p24). The latter two were designed by Juan Gómez de Mora (1586–1648).

One of Madrid's greatest architects of the late 18th century was Ventura Rodríguez (1717–85), who designed the interior of the Convento de la Encarnación and the Palacio de Liria, in a style heading towards neoclassicism. His main competitor was Italian Francesco Sabatini (1722–97), who finished the Palacio Real (p15).

Neoclassicism was best executed by Juan de Villanueva (1739–1811), who designed the building now called the Museo del Prado (p8). The 19th century saw the use of iron and glass becoming more commonplace – best exemplified by the Palacio de Cristal (p19) and

Palacio Real (p15) leads the competition

Atocha train station. The neo-Mudéjar style became the style for bullrings, with Las Ventas (p29), finished in 1934, a prime example.

In the 1920s the newly created Gran Vía (p18) provided the perfect opportunity for new buildings, and a number of Art-Deco caprices still line the boulevard.

Madrid is a relatively modern city, which means that much of it has been constructed in the last 100 years or so. Still, few recent edifices display the sparkle of 'great architecture', although the leaning Torres Puerta de Europa (p30) demonstrate some bold experimentation.

Painting

Madrid wasn't a centre of artistic production until 1561, when Felipe II moved the royal court here. Even so, the bulk of artists who lived and worked here came from elsewhere. Perhaps the most extraordinary of these was the Cretan-born Domenikos Theotokopoulos (1541–1614), popularly known as El Greco (the Greek). He chose, however, to settle in Toledo and met with relative indifference from the court of Felipe II.

The golden age of Spanish art had few figures from Madrid, although there's plenty of great art from this period to see in the city. An extensive collection of José de Ribera's (1591–1652) works are in the Prado, as are some from Bartolomé Esteban Murillo (1618–82). Francisco de Zurbarán's (1598–1664) work can be seen in the Real Academia de Bellas Artes de San Fernando (p23). The great star of this time, however, was Velázquez (1599–1660), who moved to Madrid to be court painter. His eye

Whiz through the Museo del Prado (p8)

GUY MOBERLY

for light and detail, plus the humanity that he captured in his subjects, are unmatched. His works can be seen at the Prado, including the masterpieces *Las Meninas* and *La Rendición de Breda*.

A parade of late-baroque artists working over the course of the 17th century has been loosely lumped together as the Madrid School, with some of them actually born and raised in Madrid. Antonio de Pereda (1608–78) and Fray Juan Rizi (1600–81) both have paintings in the Real Academia de Bellas Artes de San Fernando, while Madrileño Claudio Coello (1642–93) has large-scale works displayed in San Lorenzo de El Escorial (p36).

The 18th century saw Bohemian Anton Raphael Mengs (1728–79) as court painter, and it was his encouragement that inspired Francisco José de Goya y Lucientes (1746–1828) to begin a long and varied career.

Goya is recognised as Spain's greatest artist of the 18th (and even the 19th) century. His early pieces had some of the candour of Hogarth and betrayed the influence of Tiepolo. He was appointed Carlos IV's court painter in 1799, and his style grew increasingly merciless. Masterpieces at the Prado by Goya include *La Maja Vestida* and *La Maja Desnuda* (see p9), along with *Los Caprichos* (The Caprices), a biting series of 80 etchings lambasting court life.

Madrid-born Juan Gris (1887–1927) flew the cubist flag during his short life, and while the 20th century's greatest artist, Pablo Picasso (1881–1973), was born in Málaga, he did study in Madrid for a time at the Escuela de Bellas Artes de San Fernando from 1897. His most powerful work, *Guernica,* can be seen in the Centro de Arte Reina Sofía (p12).

Madrid's contemporary art scene is not as prominent as that of other European cities, but interesting exhibitions by emerging and established artists can be found in the galleries on Calle de Claudio Coello in Salamanca and in the streets around Calle de San Pedro in Cortes. This latter area is getting a reputation as a Soho (New York City) of sorts, thanks to the nearby Reina Sofía's ambitious extension and other artistic projects in the offing.

Music & Flamenco

Madrid has not contributed a great deal to the world of classical music and opera, although the tenor Placido Domingo was born in the city (his parents were *zarzuela* – light opera – performers). The family moved to Mexico when he was still a child though, so the city can't claim too much hold on his talent.

Flamenco dancers at Casa Patas (p65)

Modern popular music has been kinder to the city, with lots of rock 'n' roll blasting from the Malasaña barrio, and even a bit of indie pop in the form of well-liked band Dover. Look out for their CD *The Flame*. Hard-to-classify Miguel Bosé's *Velventina* was something of a city-wide soundtrack when we visited, and while he's not strictly a local, he has resided in the city in the past.

Although flamenco emerged in southern Spain, it is not the exclusive preserve of Andalucía. Since the mid-19th century, the best performers of flamenco have turned up at one time or another in Madrid – and many were born here. We've listed a number of venues where you can hear and see (and of course swoon at) flamenco in the Entertainment chapter (p65).

Directory

Gimme shelter: escape at the heat in the lovely Parque del Buen Retiro (p19)

RICHARD NEBESKY

ARRIVAL & DEPARTURE

Air

Madrid's **Barajas airport** (1, C3; www.aena.es) is 13km northeast of the city centre. There are three terminals: T1 mostly handles intercontinental and some European flights; T2 mostly handles domestic and Schengen-country flights with Spanish carriers; and T3 handles Iberia's Puente Aereo flights between Madrid and Barcelona, plus the odd 'regional' flight to France and Italy. Expansion work on the airport will double the number of runways and create a revolutionary new terminal by the end of 2005.

INFORMATION

Flight Information ☎ 90 235 35 70
General Inquiries ☎ 91 393 60 00

AIRPORT ACCESS

The No 8 metro line between Barajas and Nuevos Ministerios (4, D1) is the easiest way to travel from the airport to the city. The trip takes 12 minutes and from here you can easily connect to your final destination. See Metro (opposite) for general times and ticket costs.

The airport bus runs from an underground terminus at Plaza de Colón (4, E6, p26). The bus runs from 5.15am to 2am daily every 12 minutes and costs €2.50 one way. The trip takes about 30 minutes in average traffic.

A taxi to/from the airport costs around €20 to €25. Taxis queue outside all three airport terminals.

Train

Madrid's two main train stations are Atocha (2, D9) and Chamartín (2, D1) in the city's south and north respectively. Atocha is the bigger of the two, but Chamartín also serves as a departure and arrival point for many international trains. Always check you ticket beforehand.

The variety of fares and services is mind-boggling. National trains are run by **Renfe** (☎ 90 224 02 02; www.renfe.es) and tickets can be purchased by phone, online and at stations.

Bus

The main intercity bus terminal is **Estación Sur de Autobuses** (☎ 91 468 42 00; www.estaciondeauto buses.com; Calle de Méndez Álvaro), just south of the M-30 ring road. Most bus companies have a ticket office here, even if their buses depart from elsewhere. **Herranz buses** (☎ 91 896 90 28) depart from under and around Moncloa station (2, A6) for El Escorial.

The major international carrier is **Eurolines** (www.eurolines.com), which often works in tandem with Spanish carriers that depart from or arrive at Estación Sur de Autobuses.

Travel Documents

PASSPORT

Spain is one of 15 countries that are party to the Schengen Convention, and there is usually no passport control for people arriving from within the EU – although you must carry your passport or a national ID card. Citizens of the UK, Ireland and Switzerland are also covered by this arrangement.

VISA

Visas are not required by citizens of the EU, USA, Australia, Canada, New Zealand, Israel and Japan for tourist visits to Spain of up to three months. If you are a citizen of a country not listed here, check with your Spanish consulate before you travel, as you may need a specific visa. If you intend to stay for more than three months you must apply for a resident's card.

Customs & Duty Free

From outside the EU, you can bring in one bottle of spirits, one bottle of wine, 50mL of perfume and 200 ciggies. From an EU country (with duty paid) you can bring in 90L of wine, 10L of spirits, unlimited perfume and 800 ciggies, and really make a party of it.

Left Luggage

The airport's *consigna* (left luggage) offices are in T1 (near the bus stop and taxi stand) and T2 (near the metro entrance). Both are open 24 hours and charge €2.60 for the first 24 hours. Estación Sur de Autobuses operates a **left-luggage office** (☉ 6.30am-midnight) near where the buses exit the station.

GETTING AROUND

Madrid's public transport system is reliable, efficient and user friendly. The metro is by far the best way to get around town; it has stops close to most places of interest, new stops are being added all the time and it doesn't smell like an underground urinal. The metro is complemented by the Cercanías suburban rail system, and an extensive network of local buses.

The main transport system finishes at around 1.30am, which means you'll sometimes need to use taxis to get the most out of Madrid's famed nightlife. And Madrid being Madrid, it can be harder to get a taxi at 4am than 4pm! Maps of Madrid's transport network are available from tourist offices, train and metro stations, and the airport.

In this book, the nearest metro or Cercanías stations are noted after the Ⓜ or Ⓡ in each listing.

Travel Passes

Single and 10-trip passes can be used on both buses and the metro; a single trip costs €1.15 and a Metrobús ticket (valid for 10 trips) costs €5.80.

Monthly or season passes *(abonos)* are only worth buying if you are staying long term and using local transport frequently. You'll also need an ID card *(carnet)*, available from metro stations and tobacconists. Take a passport-sized photo and your passport. A monthly ticket for central Madrid (Zona A) costs €37.15 and is valid for unlimited travel on buses, the metro and Cercanías trains.

Metro

Madrid's excellent **metro system** (☎ 90 244 44 03; www.metromad rid.es) has 13 colour-coded lines (with extra stops being added all the time) and runs from about 6am to 1.30am daily. You can buy tickets from staffed kiosks or machines at the stations. Only some of the newer stations have wheelchair access.

Bus

Buses run by **Empresa Municipal de Transportes de Madrid** (EMT; ☎ 91 406 99 00; www.ctm-mad rid.es) travel regularly along more than 100 lines, between 6.30am and 11.30pm daily. About half of the buses are *piso bajo* types, meaning they are wheelchair friendly.

Cercanías

These short-range regional trains are handy for making north–south trips between Chamartín and Atocha stations, and for day trips to places such as El Escorial. As this system is operated by Renfe, the national rail network, tickets (single trip €1.05) are not valid on buses or the metro, although most international rail passes are valid.

Taxi

Madrid's taxis (white with a diagonal red stripe) are plentiful and good value compared to other European cities. Make sure the driver turns the meter on; flag fall is €1.65 plus 75c per km (90c between 10pm and 6am). On public holidays it's 90c per km (€1 between 10pm and 6am). Supplementary charges include: €4.20 to/from the airport, €2.20 from cab ranks at train and bus stations, €2.20 for travelling to/from Parque Juan Carlos I, and a special charge on Christmas Eve and New Year's Eve.

A green light on the roof, or a sign displayed behind the windscreen with the word *'libre'*, means the taxi is available. You can book taxis by calling the following numbers: ☎ 91 405 12 13, 91 404 90 00, 91 445 90 08 or ☎ 91 447 51 80.

Car & Motorcycle

On a short trip to Madrid, you're unlikely to need your own wheels, and the traffic congestion, seemingly endless roadworks in the city centre and parking restrictions (not to mention the environmental impact) will not make driving here a pleasant experience. The risk of car theft is another deterrent. Motorcycles and scooters are popular modes of transport, but Madrid is not the place to learn how to ride them! However, if you do need to hire a vehicle, you could try:

Avis (3, C1; ☎ 90 213 55 31, 91 547 20 48; Gran Vía 60; Ⓜ Santo Domingo)

Europcar (4, A6; ☎ 90 210 50 30, 91 541 88 92; Calle de San Leonardo 8; Ⓜ Plaza de España)

Hertz (4, A6; ☎ 90 240 24 05, 91 372 93 00; Edificio de España, Plaza de España; Ⓜ Plaza de España)

PRACTICALITIES
Climate & When to Go

Madrid's continental climate brings with it scorching hot summers and dry, cold winters. Locals say *'nueve meses de invierno y tres de infierno'* (nine months of winter and three months of hell). This is a slight exaggeration, but at its worst, Madrid can be nastily cold and infernally hot.

July and August are hottest, with temperatures frequently over 30°C and sometimes over 40°C. In winter, temperatures can plummet to freezing at night and might only nudge 10°C during the day. Late April and May are lovely times to visit, as are September and early October (although this month can be rainy). February can be surprisingly nice, with blue skies and sun. March is often unpredictable, and early April can be wet.

The combination of tourists and business travellers visiting Madrid means that hotels are busy for much of the year. The city is especially crowded during Easter, Christmas holidays and local festivals. Many Madrileños take holidays in August, which means that the city is noticeably less crowded, and many businesses are open for reduced hours or close altogether at this time.

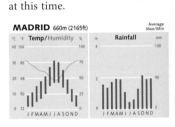

Disabled Travellers

In Madrid there are some buses and metro stations adapted for wheelchairs. The streets, however, have not been designed with impaired mobility in mind. Many of the older museums don't have wheelchair access, although the 'big three' museums have been kitted out. Look for the Ⓖ listed with individual reviews. With the use of this symbol, we've indicated the degree to which the sight meets the needs of disabled travellers, ranging from limited to excellent. Limited means that some access is available (such as a ramp), but that stairs are also present, while excellent means that the building affords maximum accessibility.

Radio-Teléfono Taxi (☎ 91 547 82 00, 91 547 86 00) runs taxis for the disabled. Generally, if you call any taxi company and ask for a *eurotaxi* you should be sent one adapted for wheelchair users. The Ayuntamiento de Madrid publishes a *Guía de Accesibilidad* which contains information on disabled access to everything from the city's cinemas through to its public service buildings.

Discounts

Concessions (of up to 50%) are available for youths, students and seniors over 65 years (with identification) at most attractions and on some transport. Generally, when we quote concession prices in this guide, it's for the aforementioned people. The most widely recognised student and youth cards are the International Student Identity Card (ISIC) and the Carnet Joven Europeo (Euro <26 card). It's worth carrying photo ID and flashing it wherever possible to see what discounts (which are not always advertised) are available.

Electricity

Voltage	220V
Frequency	50Hz
Cycle	AC
Plugs	two round pins

Embassies

Australia (4, C2; ☎ 91 441 60 25; www.spain.embassy.gov.au; Plaza del Descubridor Diego de Ordás 3; Ⓜ Ríos Rosas)

France (3, J2; ☎ 91 423 89 00; www.ambafrance-es.org not in English; Calle de Salustiano Olózaga 9; Ⓜ Retiro)

UK (4, E5; ☎ 91 700 82 00; www.ukinspain.com; Calle de Fernando el Santo 16; Ⓜ Colón)

USA (4, F4; ☎ 91 587 22 00; www.embusa.es; Calle de Serrano 75; Ⓜ Núñez de Balboa)

Emergencies

Generally speaking, Madrid is a safe city, although it's always wise to keep a lookout for pickpockets on the metro and at major tourist attractions.

Never leave anything in your car and don't get a hire car that has marking identifying it as such. Foreign number plates make you even more vulnerable.

Ambulance ☎ 061

EU standard emergency number ☎ 112

Fire Brigade (Bomberos) ☎ 080

Local Police ☎ 092

Military Police ☎ 062

National Police ☎ 091

Rape Crisis ☎ 91 574 01 10 (⏲ 10am-2pm & 4-7pm Mon-Thu, 10am-4pm Fri)

Fitness

Despite their love of food and drink, Madrileños make looking good an art form, and some are prepared to exercise to keep themselves easy on the eye. The city itself, with its parks, pools, gyms and golf courses, is a good place to keep your fitness regimen going.

GYM

Many of Madrid's deluxe and top-end hotels have work-out facilities for guests. Grab a list of *polideportivos* (sports centres) that have gyms from one of the tourist offices. The Chueca neighbourhood has a handful of gay-friendly gyms that accept casual visitors. Public gyms and indoor pools (normally for lap swimming only) are scattered throughout Madrid. They generally charge a modest fee of €4 to €6 for one-day admission. If you're looking for fewer crowds, head to one of Madrid's privately owned health centres, where you will pay around €10 for a day's admission.

JOGGING
Madrid's parks have plenty of paths that can be used by joggers. Our favourite is the Campo del Moro (p26), not just for its beauty, but also because it seems relatively undiscovered. Other parks that are popular with joggers include the Retiro (p19), which has a designated jogging path, and the Casa de Campo (p26), which is at its best early in the morning.

SWIMMING
Outdoor pools are open from June to September in several locations. During the rest of the year, indoor pools operate, as do some private pools that allow casual visits. See p31 for details of Madrid's *hammam* (hot baths).

Hotel Emperador (3, C2; ☎ 91 547 28 00; Gran Vía 53; admission from €25; Ⓜ Gran Vía, Santo Domingo) Probably the city's swankiest place to swim, this pool is located on the rooftop and has marvellous views of the city. Nonguests are allowed to swim here.

Piscinas Casa de Campo (2, A7; ☎ 91 463 00 50; Avenida del Ángel, Casa de Campo; adult €4; ☺ 11.30am-9pm summer, 9am-noon, 3-7pm & 9-10pm winter; Ⓜ Lago) Has a great vibe, with all types jostling for space – families, preening narcissists, fitness fanatics and old folks, all enjoying a dip and a bit of sun (topless permitted).

Gay & Lesbian Travellers
Madrid is very much a 'live and let live' city, and the gay and lesbian scene is out, loud and proud. Centred in the Chueca neighbourhood, but certainly not ghetto-ised, gay life here does not warrant furtive secrecy or segregation. In fact, it's fairly standard to see straight people in gay bars and clubs and gay people anywhere and everywhere. In Chueca though, you'll find bars, clubs, restaurants, shops and hotels that specifically cater to gay and lesbian customers.

Gay and lesbian sex are both legal in Spain and the age of consent is 16 years, the same as for heterosexuals.

At the time of writing a draft bill had been approved by the lower house of parliament in Spain and was awaiting some rubber-stamping by the senate, thus making Spain Europe's third country to recognise gay marriage and the first to legalise gay adoption of children.

INFORMATION & ORGANISATIONS
The **Colectivo de Gais y Lesbianas de Madrid** (Cogam; 3, F1; ☎ 91 522 45 17; www.cogam.org in Spanish; Calle de Fuencarral 37; Ⓜ Gran Vía) has an information office and social centre and an information line (☎ 91 523 00 70). **Fundación Triángulo** (4, C4; ☎ 91 593 05 40; www.fundaciontriangulo.es; Calle de Eloy Gonzalo 25; Ⓜ Iglesia) is another source of information on gay issues. Free publications worth picking up from the Chueca area include *Shanguide* and *Mapa Gaya de Madrid*, which you can find at the Berkana bookshop (p41) and all round Chueca's gay-friendly businesses. The monthly *MENsual* (€4) is available at newsstands and online at www.mensual.com (in Spanish).

Health
IMMUNISATIONS

There are no vaccination requirements for those entering Spain, although you may need to show proof of vaccination if you're coming from an area where yellow fever is endemic (Africa and South America).

MEDICAL SERVICES

Travel insurance is advisable to cover any medical treatment you may need while in Madrid. Spain has reciprocal health agreements with other EU countries. Citizens of those countries need to get hold of an E111 form from their national health body. If you should require medical help you will need to present this, plus photocopies of the form and your national health card. Places to seek medical treatment include:

Anglo-American Medical Unit
(2, D7; ☎ 91 435 18 23; Calle del Conde de Aranda 1; ⏰ 9am-8pm Mon-Fri; Ⓜ Retiro) A private clinic where staff speak English.

Hospital General Gregorio Marañon (2, E7; ☎ 91 586 80 00; Calle del Doctor Esquerdo; Ⓜ Sáinz de Baranda) One of the city's main hospitals, with a 24-hour emergency department.

DENTAL SERVICES

If you chip a tooth or require emergency treatment (in English), head to **Clinica Dental Cisne** (4, B4; ☎ 91 446 32 21; Calle de Magallanes 18).

PHARMACIES

At least one pharmacy is open 24 hours per day in each district of Madrid. They mostly operate on a rota and details appear daily in *El País* and other papers, or you can call ☎ 010. The following pharmacies are open 24 hours:

Farmacia del Globo (3, F5; ☎ 91 369 20 00; Plaza de Antón Martín 46; Ⓜ Antón Martín)

Farmacia Velázquez (4, F5; ☎ 91 575 60 28; Calle de Velázquez 70; Ⓜ Velázquez)

Real Farmacia de la Reina (3, C4; ☎ 91 548 00 14; Calle Mayor 59; Ⓜ Ópera)

Holidays

1 January	New Year's Day
6 January	Epiphany or Three Kings' Day
March–April	Good Thursday
March–April	Good Friday
1 May	Labour Day
2 May	El Dos de Mayo
15 August	Feast of the Assumption
12 October	Spanish National Holiday
1 November	All Saints' Day
8 December	Feast of the Immaculate Conception
25 December	Christmas Day

Internet

Madrid has many Internet cafés, ranging in size from veritable telecommunications palaces with dozens of terminals to small operations with a handful of terminals. Many of the larger places to stay have facilities for guests for free or for a minimal fee, with connections available from your room.

INTERNET ACCESS

3w.com (3, D3; Calle de Tetuán 3; per 30mins 70c; ⏰ 9am-midnight Mon-Sat, 11am-midnight Sun; Ⓜ Sol)

BBiGG (3, F3; ☎ 91 531 23 64; www.bbigg.com; Calle de Alcalá 21; per hr €2; ⏰ 9.30am-midnight; Ⓜ Gran Vía, Sevilla)

Telefónica (3, E2; Gran Vía 30; per hr €1.50; ☻ 10am-10pm; Ⓜ Gran Vía)

USEFUL WEBSITES

The Lonely Planet website (www .lonelyplanet.com) offers a speedy link to many of Madrid's websites. Others to try include:

Ayuntamiento de Madrid www .munimadrid.es

Comunidad de Madrid www.co madrid.es in Spanish

Descubre Madrid www.descubre madrid.com

Metro de Madrid www.metro madrid.es

Renfe www.renfe.es

Lost Property

Airport ☎ 91 393 61 19

EMT buses ☎ 91 406 88 43

Main lost property office (Negociado de Objetos Perdidos – for Metro) ☎ 91 588 43 48

Renfe ☎ 91 902 24 02 02

Metric System

Spain uses the metric system. Decimal points are indicated with commas and thousands with points.

TEMPERATURE

$°C = (°F - 32) ÷ 1.8$
$°F = (°C × 1.8) + 32$

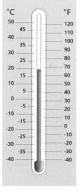

	°C	°F

DISTANCE
1in = 2.54cm
1cm = 0.39in
1m = 3.3ft = 1.1yd
1ft = 0.3m
1km = 0.62 miles
1 mile = 1.6km

WEIGHT
1kg = 2.2lb
1lb = 0.45kg
1g = 0.04oz
1oz = 28g

VOLUME
1L = 0.26 US gallons
1 US gallon = 3.8L
1L = 0.22 imperial gallons
1 imperial gallon = 4.55L

Money
ATMS

Multilingual ATMs *(telebancos)* are common throughout Madrid, and as long as you're connected to the Cirrus or Maestro network, you're good to go. It usually works out cheaper than exchanging travellers cheques too, but check first with your bank at home for associated charges.

CURRENCY

The unit of currency is the euro. Notes come in denominations of €500, €200, €100, €50, €20, €10 and €5. Coins come in denominations of €2 and €1, plus 50c, 20c, 10c, 5c, 2c and 1c.

CREDIT CARDS

Credit cards are widely accepted throughout the city. Some places will want to see another form of photo ID, such as a passport or driving licence, but your signature will rarely be checked. For 24-hour card cancellations or assistance, call:

American Express ☎ 90 237 56 37

Diners Club ☎ 90 240 11 12

MasterCard/Eurocard ☎ 90 097 12 31

Visa ☎ 90 099 12 16

CHANGING MONEY

You can change cash or travellers cheques at most banks (Madrid is swarming with them) and at exchange offices, bus and train stations and the airport. Banks tend to offer the best rates, and most have ATMs. Exchange offices (mostly clustered around the Plaza de la Puerta del Sol and along Gran Vía) are usually indicated by the word *cambio* (exchange) and offer longer opening hours and quicker service but have poorer exchange rates. Travellers cheques usually bring a slightly better rate than cash, but always check commissions.

Newspapers & Magazines

Madrid's main newspapers are *El País* and *El Mundo*. International newspapers, which include the *International Herald Tribune,* are available at newsstands around central Madrid, especially along Gran Vía and around Plaza de la Puerta del Sol. The *Guía del Ocio* (€1) is a must-read for anyone wanting to sample Madrid's entertainment options, and can be found at any newsstand. *Shangay* is Madrid's free gay paper and is available in many shops and bars, especially around the Chueca neighbourhood. *In Madrid* is a free English-language newspaper with good entertainment listings and classifieds. You can find it in bars and shops around the city.

Opening Hours

Following is a guide to typical opening hours in Madrid; check individual listings for details. Many shops close on Sunday, public holidays and for a few weeks in August. Virtually all museums close on Monday, and many attractions are open shorter hours (or closed) in August.

Banks 8.30am-2pm Mon-Fri; some also open 4-7pm Thu & 9am-1pm Sat

Central post office 8.30am-9.30pm Mon-Sat; some branches open 8.30am-8.30pm Mon-Fri & 9.30am-1pm Sat, but most open only 8am-2pm, Mon-Fri

Offices 9am-2pm & 5-8pm Mon-Fri

Restaurants noon-4pm & 8pm-midnight, or to after midnight Fri & Sat

Shops 10am-2pm & 5-8pm Mon-Fri; some big stores don't close for siesta

Post

Madrid's postal service is reliable and efficient. The main post office is in the **Palacio de Comunicaciones** (p29). At the time of writing, there were plans afoot to turn this into the town hall *(ayuntamiento)* and move the post office nearby.

Stamps are sold at most *estancos* (tobacconists – look for the sign with 'Tabacos' written in yellow letters on a maroon background), as well as at post offices *(correos)*.

POSTAL RATES

Postage on a standard postcard or letter weighing up to 20g costs 28c within Spain, 53c within Europe, and 78c to the Americas and Australasia.

Radio

BBC World Service (6195kHz, 9410kHz & 15,485kHz) International news and features; station depends on time of day.

Onda Cero (98FM) Pop and rock.

RNE1 (88.2FM) General interest and current affairs.

Sinfo Radio (104.3FM) Classical music.

Voice of America (6040kHz, 9760kHz & 15,205kHz) Can be found on shortwave frequencies.

Telephone

The ubiquitous blue payphones are easy to use for both domestic and international calls. They accept coins, phonecards *(tarjetas telefónicas)* and sometimes credit cards.

PHONECARDS

Tarjetas telefónicas are sold at post offices, *estancos* and many newsstands; they come in denominations of €6 and €12.

MOBILE PHONES

Spain uses the GSM cellular *(movil)* phone system, which works with most phones except those sold in the USA and Japan. To use your phone, you'll need to set up a global roaming service with your service provider before you leave home, or you can buy a Spanish SIM card from around €25.

COUNTRY & CITY CODES

The city code is an integral part of the number and must always be dialled, whether calling from next door or abroad. The codes are:

Spain ☎ 34

Madrid ☎ 91

USEFUL NUMBERS

International Directory Inquiries ☎ 11825

International Operator Europe/ North Africa ☎ 1008

International Operator rest of the world ☎ 1005

Local Directory Inquiries ☎ 1009

National Directory Inquiries ☎ 11818

Reverse-charge (collect) ☎ 900 (+ code of the country you are calling)

TV

State-run TVE1 and La 2 broadcast a combination of progovernment news, good arts programmes and films. Antena 3 and Tele 5 are commercial stations sending out woeful Latin American soaps and 'all tits and teeth' variety shows. Canal Plus is a pay channel mostly devoted to film and football. Many hotels have access to cable TV stations.

Time

Madrid is one hour ahead of GMT/UTC and two hours ahead during daylight savings. Daylight savings is observed for around seven months from the last Sunday in March to the last Sunday in October. Spaniards use the 24-hour clock for official business (timetables etc), but often in daily conversation switch to the 12-hour version.

Tipping

The law stipulates that restaurants include service charges in menu prices, so tipping is very much discretionary. Many people leave small change at bars and cafés (5% is plenty). Hotel porters will be happy with €1 and taxi drivers OK with a round-up.

Toilets

Public toilets are not common in Madrid. If you get caught short while sightseeing, you can pop into a bar or café, although some places might like you to buy a drink first.

Tourist Information

The tourist offices in the city have friendly staff who speak English (among other languages) and can provide maps and information about Madrid and its environs. The Patronato Municipal de Turismo specialises in Madrid-only information. Bright yellow kiosks are established in summer around well-touristed city points, with multilingual staff. There are also information points in Atocha and Chamartín stations.

Barajas airport (1, C3; ☎ 91 305 86 56; ground fl, T1; ☺ 8am-8pm)

Main Tourist Office (Oficina de Turismo Duque de Medinaceli; 3, G4; ☎ 91 429 37 05; Calle del Duque de Medinaceli 2; ☺ 9am-7pm Mon-Sat, to 3pm Sun & hols; Ⓜ Banco de España)

Patronato Municipal de Turismo (3, D4; ☎ 91 588 16 36; inforturismo@munimadrid.es; Plaza Mayor 3; ☺ 10am-8pm Mon-Sat, to 3pm Sun & hols; Ⓜ Sol)

Women Travellers

Female visitors to Madrid will get the feeling that women's rights are respected here. Lone women walking around late at night should encounter little troublesome attention, although the Lavapiés neighbourhood is best avoided in these circumstances.

Tampons and the contraceptive pill are widely available in Madrid at pharmacies.

LANGUAGE

It's well worth the effort to try a few phrases in Spanish during your stay in Madrid, as English is not as widely spoken as many travellers may think. For an in-depth guide to the language, get a copy of Lonely Planet's Spanish phrasebook.

Basics

Hello.	*¡Hola!*
Goodbye.	*¡Adiós!*
Yes.	*Sí.*
No.	*No.*

Please.	*Por favor.*
Thank you.	*Gracias.*
You're welcome.	*De nada.*
Excuse me.	*Perdón.*
Sorry/Excuse me.	*Lo siento/ Discúlpeme.*
Do you speak English?	*¿Habla inglés?*
I don't understand.	*No entiendo.*
How much is it?	*¿Cuánto cuesta esto?*

Emergencies

Help!	*¡Socorro!*
Call a doctor!	*¡Llame a un doctor!*
Call the police!	*¡Llame a la policía!*
Where are the toilets?	*¿Dónde están los servicios?*
Go away!	*¡Váyase!*
I'm lost (m/f).	*Estoy perdido/a.*

Index

EATING

SLEEPING

SHOPPING

Sights Index

FEATURES

Las Bravas	*Eating*
Alphaville	*Entertainment*
Antik Café	*Drinking*
Palacio Real	*Highlights*
Camper	*Shopping*
Real Madrid	*Sights/Activities*
Hotel Miau	*Sleeping*

AREAS

	Beach, Desert
	Building
	Land
	Mall
	Other Area
	Park/Cemetery
	Sports
	Urban

HYDROGRAPHY

	River, Creek
	Intermittent River
	Canal
	Swamp
	Water

BOUNDARIES

	State, Provincial
	Regional, Suburb
	Ancient Wall

ROUTES

	Tollway
	Freeway
	Primary Road
	Secondary Road
	Tertiary Road
	Lane
	Under Construction
	One-Way Street
	Unsealed Road
	Mall/Steps
	Tunnel
	Walking Path
	Walking Trail/Track
	Pedestrian Overpass
	Walking Tour

TRANSPORT

	Airport, Airfield
	Bus Route
	Cycling, Bicycle Path
	General Transport
	Metro
	Monorail
	Rail
	Taxi Rank
	Tram

SYMBOLS

	Bank, ATM
	Buddhist
	Castle, Fortress
	Christian
	Diving, Snorkeling
	Embassy, Consulate
	Hospital, Clinic
	Information
	Internet Access
	Islamic
	Jewish
	Lighthouse
	Lookout
	Monument
	Mountain, Volcano
	National Park
	Parking Area
	Petrol Station
	Picnic Area
	Point of Interest
	Police Station
	Post Office
	Ruin
	Telephone
	Toilets
	Zoo, Bird Sanctuary

24/7 travel advice
www.lonelyplanet.com